Man Of Compassion –
Man Of Prayer
*The guiding hand of God
in the life of John Harris*

Man Of Compassion – Man Of Prayer
The guiding hand of God in the life of John Harris

Doreen Sharp

paternoster
Lifestyle

For leprosy patients and workers everywhere

Contents

Contents

Foreword

I think John Harris might have spelt this 'forward'! He would not have wanted us to spend much time looking back on his past and would have allowed it only to serve as encouragement to go on in the service of Christ for our own generation. John took delight in writing poems, mainly based on the Psalms, but on his (reluctant) retirement from The Leprosy Mission, it was his wife, Elsie, who wrote a poem for him. It was entitled 'Retired'

> Retired, so they say
> On Mission page and pension list.
> Formal farewells, and flower bouquet.
> Retired.
>
> Re-tyred, *He* says.
> For mileage new in service lowly, loyal, true,
> And to His praise.
> Occupy until I come.
> Finish your course with joy,
> Looking unto Jesus
> Until the race is finished and the crown is won.

I began to know John when I was a young minister with a keen personal interest in the subject of revival. Knowing he had personal knowledge of the Congo revival of 1953, I tried hard to 'pump' him for some more information. But instead of regaling me with stories old and new about it, he simply replied over and over, 'We must pray and prepare for the *next* one, brother.' That future look with its present urgency and impetus was always with John: a man of vision and a man of passion, a man of prayer and of single-minded obedience.

Jesus' beatitude, 'Blessed are the pure in heart' is, the commentators agree, a reference more to single-mindedness than to morality, indicating the passion for God that wills one thing. John was a living and life-long illustration of that, He desired fervently that God should be served with all his ransomed powers and that He should have all the glory. Jesus' promise 'For they shall see God' is even now being fulfilled in John's life in heaven.

When home in the UK with Elsie, and here in Nottingham to spend time with their daughter Lois and her husband Richard and the grandchildren, John would take an unobtrusive back seat in the Sunday congregation at Cornerstone, but for me his presence was luminous with encouragement. He was quite simply the most prayerful man I have ever known and the knowledge that Cornerstone and myself were on his prayer-list for daily prayer was for me the promise of God that He was with us and would bless us if we were faithful. That continues to be the case as Elsie lives here in retirement, prayerfully involved in

Cornerstone's ongoing life, and at the centre of our own world-mission involvement.

John and Elsie were convinced that God had given them a ministry of intercession. For them prayer was not about the work, it was part of the work. Not only at home and as part of their regular 'Quiet Times' and prayer-days together but at many other times short and long, on long car journeys for instance, or when he was awake in the night, the time would be 'redeemed' with prayer. And the prayer was no light or casual thing either.

On one occasion I asked John to lead a prayer meeting at our church here. I still cherish the memory. It was a military operation! There was a list of people, places, and situations that needed the urgent prayers of God's people and we were there for precisely that. People were expected to pray but they had better be quick about it because there was much to be done in the heavenly places that night. The separate prayer times were timed to the second and then it was on to the next. The (mainly young) people had never quite been directed in that manner before. But it certainly stirred them up to see prayer as the King's business and I distinctly remember the irritated sounds of some who had been about to pray aloud but 'missed it' because they had let the silence go on for a few seconds. The sergeant-major wasn't waiting for anyone; it was their business to look sharp and get on with it.

John's daughter Lois remembers as a child waking in the middle of the night more than once and going for water only to find her father on his knees in the living room while the others were sleeping. If he had a brief nap in the ever-busy day it would be sitting in the chair with a bunch of keys in his hand so that when they dropped to the floor he would wake up and could resume work! He was never idle and even while shaving he would set himself to learn a few texts of Scripture in some local dialect so that he could communicate the gospel to some extent.

I longed for John to write a full account of his life but I think he would have needed some angelic Boswell who could eavesdrop on every conversation. John was so averse to talking of himself that any autobiography would have become a clarion-call to the reader to stop reading, get up and do something! Certainly it would have been more about his Lord than himself.

When all is said and done (and written), John's life is recorded in heaven and only a small part of it can be made known on earth. But it is being told on earth in the ongoing lives of hundreds and of thousands who have been helped by John medically or spiritually or both. God is still gathering up the glory of uncounted prayers and their fruit, of long-forgotten conversations and their effect, and in glory is still saying to this man, 'Well done, good and faithful servant'.

Peter Lewis,
The Cornerstone Evangelical Church,
Nottingham.

Introduction

Among my early memories of my brother John is the time when he asked me to be his photographer's assistant. He was five years older than me, and even at the age of twelve he was motivated by the 'never do anything by half-measures' motto which characterized his life. His studio for developing his photographs was a very small and dingy room in the basement of our home in St John's Wood. I remember the feeling of privilege at being invited to help in such vital and skilled work, but I also remember the terrible sense of failure when I inadvertently let in some light by opening the door at the wrong moment. The photographer was extremely annoyed, and my sense of pride was severely dented.

Later, happier memories of my brother are of someone who lived in an atmosphere of communion with God. He always took a lively interest in family members of all generations, and was quick to note down any special needs for prayer. He was never afraid to speak out when he felt a person could be helped by a word of advice, or a word of warning to keep them on the Christian path. He was someone who, after one meeting, left you with a renewed desire to walk more closely with the Lord.

Not long after John's sudden death in 1995 I felt a strong desire, I believe God-given, to chronicle his life. There was a vital message of prayer and commitment to pass on. I would hope that God might use this book about His faithful servant to challenge others to follow Him.

There are many people among my family and friends who have given me encouragement during the writing of this book. Debra Chand of The Leprosy Mission is the one who emboldened me to take the plunge. Those who replied to my request for memories are named in the book, and I greatly value their contributions in helping to give a true and balanced picture of John's life. One of my main sources of inspiration was my sister-in-law, Elsie. Soon after John's death she wrote down an account of their years together and I have relied much on this, as I have on her careful reading of the manuscript to check for accuracy.

I am grateful, too, for the literary skills of Sarah Lewis and Anne Spredbury in reading the manuscript and making critical comments. Anne painstakingly gave help with the first few chapters until she became ill. She is now with the Lord.

I am indebted to Monarch Books for granting permission to use extracts from the chapter about John's death entitled 'Elsie's Story' in *Pathway Through Grief*, edited by Jean Watson.

In this my first experience of writing a book for publication, Nancy Lush and Jill Morris of Paternoster Publishing have been most helpful and understanding. I am grateful for all their detailed work, and that of others involved in preparations for publishing.

In compiling this book I have learned many things about John that I never knew before. I pray that others will benefit from the reading, as I have done from the writing.

1

Firm Foundations

One evening in late 1994, a missionary doctor was making his way home to the Nyankunde Medical Centre. He had had a tiring journey by road and boat under the tropical sun. Travelling conditions in north-east Zaire were tough. He could not reach his destination that evening, so the home of missionary Maizie Smyth in the interior town of Kisangani was a welcome place to spend the night. As Maizie greeted the doctor she felt sure that after a meal and a shower he would want to rest. There was just one visit she must make, to a sick Nepali man who worked for a family of Indian Christians. The man knew neither Swahili nor French, the languages spoken locally, and no one had visited him. The doctor put the thought of rest aside and said he would go along with Maizie. He would enjoy the walk.

Entering the room first, Maizie saw the sick man groaning and trying to say how ill he felt. Somehow she conveyed to him that there was a doctor with her who might be able to help. Then the doctor came into the room and greeted the man in his own language! Maizie had no idea that he spoke Nepali. The effect was immediate, and the lonely stranger's condition improved remarkably. The doctor spent the next hour bringing comfort to the young Nepali, speaking from the heart about his Lord. Maizie could only wonder silently, 'Think of it, one sick stranger in the heart of Africa and the Lord directs John to his bedside.' Recounting the incident to friends at home, she wrote, 'I praise God for the life of John.'

Within a few months the doctor, John Harris, went to be with Christ. How had God woven the strands of this life to make it so sensitive to His leading? The pattern had begun to take shape many years before, in London.

★ ★ ★ ★ ★

John's father, Herbert Harris (known to his family as Bertie), had married his childhood sweetheart, Marie Lawson, in 1906. Marie's father had been a pioneer, being involved especially in the construction of bicycles and in the introduction of the first Daimler cars from the continent. They had seven children. Baby Ruth was born first, in 1907, followed by Alec in 1908, Vincent in 1910, Monica in 1912, Norman in 1913, Annette in 1916 and Wendy in 1919. Ruth remembers her twelfth birthday, spent with her sister Monica in an aunt and uncle's home, well, as on that day news came of her mother's death. Little Wendy was only one week old. Bertie was shattered. He came from a family of eleven, so one of his unmarried sisters came to help him care for his motherless children. Auntie Hope, a cheerful and efficient lady, did her best for eighteen months to make up for the loss of their much-loved mother. But Bertie prayed he would find another wife to cherish the whole family. This prayer was answered in Rose Secrett.

Rose's mother had died when Rose was seventeen. As the only girl in a family of seven, caring for her father and brothers became her responsibility. Before she became

Photo: Pat Thomas
The Harris family in 1985, on the occasion of
Rose Harris's 90th birthday.

Back Row, from left: Wendy, Doreen, Patricia, Margaret, Tricia (daughter of Alec, who was in South Africa), Norman.
Front row, from left: Annette, Rosemary, Vincent, Rose, John (on ground), Pamela, Ruth, Monica.

engaged to Bertie she had been to a meeting of the China Inland Mission (CIM). There they had appealed for nurses and other medical workers to serve in China. She had gone home and told her father that she wanted to train as a nurse and become a missionary there! Her father had had other ideas. Rose did not dispute his decision, but God saw and remembered her willingness to serve Him abroad. Many years later, one of her daughters described her life as a 'mission to missionaries'. Five members of her family became missionaries overseas, including one to China. Other family members were involved in various ways with mission at home. She gave tremendous support to each one, through her personal letters and her care for those on furlough.

In 1921 Bertie brought Rose, his new bride, to the family home at 18 Marlborough Hill, St John's Wood, London, where her adjustment to married life included the care of seven children under fifteen. She went on to have six children herself. Rosemary was born first, in 1922, then John Rupert in 1924, Pamela in 1925, Patricia in 1928, myself in 1930 and Margaret in 1932. It was a well-known secret in the family that Rose, having cared for her six brothers, had a special place in her heart for boys. John Rupert was no exception. (As a child, John was known as Rupert, but in 1949 he had an experience of great blessing from the Lord. From that time on, he marked this stage in his Christian life by being called John.) The girls were, of course, much loved, but Rose would have considered another boy a bonus! The two families were brought up as one. No mention was made of half-brothers and sisters.

*   *   *   *   *

Number 18's nursery was therefore alive with children of all ages. It was not a large room, but the children found plenty to do. As well as rubber and wooden bricks and other toys of the early 1900s, there was a swing that could be let down from the ceiling. One of the small 'swingers' remembers the sense of achievement when she went so high that she touched the ceiling, on one side with her head and on the other side with her feet. At night two folding beds were let down, and sometimes there was a cot as well. The room also contained a bookcase that could be reversed and turned into a bed. The nursery was a place where learning and loving and joys and upsets mixed naturally with plenty of fun. On one wall was a picture of a boy scout, gazing into the distance. Standing behind him, Jesus was depicted with His hands on the boy's shoulders. Underneath were the words from 2 Timothy 2:3, 'Thou therefore endure hardness, as a good soldier of Jesus Christ.'(KJV) As far as the young John was concerned this picture was perhaps the most significant object in the nursery. It foreshadowed the mandate of his life.

As the children grew older they overflowed into two rooms at the top of the house, one for boys and one for girls. There was no heating, no electricity and only candles for lighting. In winter it could be so cold that ice had to be broken on the basin of water before the children could wash their faces. The house had a small garden with trees to climb, but the main outdoor attraction was the five grass tennis courts across the road. Bertie Harris rented these for what was a small sum by today's standards. The children spent many happy hours playing on the space the courts provided, with tennis proving a popular sport. The Harrises made the courts available for their church's young people's weekly club. The popularity of this was due, in part, to the delicious teas with home-made cakes that Rose provided after the games.

★ ★ ★ ★ ★

One family event that was anticipated with great eagerness was the family holiday in August, when Bertie rented a house in Overstrand, Norfolk, for five weeks. He transported all those still living at home to this clifftop paradise, overlooking a sandy beach. The preparations for this annual exodus were mammoth. For Rose and Esther, the family's faithful live-in helper, there was the packing of clothes for around ten people. The children were allowed a small case each, and these were packed and repacked for weeks beforehand. A small bus came to the door to take the family and the canary in his cage, together with piles of trunks and other luggage, to Liverpool Street station. The children loved the excitement of the train journey and everyone vyed for a place near the window so that they could be the first to shout, 'I've seen the sea!' The activities of the Children's Special Service Mission were greatly enjoyed and memories abound of tide fights, sausage sizzles and scavenger hunts. Building and decorating a beach pulpit gave creative work to many willing helpers. But the war put an end to these idyllic times.

★   ★   ★   ★   ★

Bertie worked tirelessly to provide for his large family. He made his children's education a major part of his responsibility as a father. If there was proof that an activity was educational, finance was found for it. Bertie's prayer was that each one of his children would give back in service to God what had been invested in their education. In the home a very strict rein was kept on the spending of money. Luxuries were not a part of daily living. Every penny of pocket money had to be accounted for in a book, and this included a tithe for God's work. Ruth remembers the time when four pence was the weekly sum received. Of this, one penny went to Dr Barnado's homes for children, one into a savings account and the remaining two could be spent as desired.

God's name was honoured at number 18, and the Bible was taught. Discipline was strict and punishment meted out fairly, at least in the eyes of the parents! Penalties included standing in the corner for long periods, or writing out a hundred lines. These usually began, 'I must not . . .' Some of the children, who were ambidextrous, perfected the skill of writing these lists with two pens at once.

Bertie and Rose were devoted members of Mount Zion Strict Baptist Church, near Lord's Cricket Ground. Bertie was organist and taught in the Sunday school, which John attended from an early age. Sunday was spent mainly in church or walking the mile there and back. Morning Sunday school was followed by the church service. Then it was home to lunch, which consisted mainly of cold meat and salad so that there would be the minimum amount of cooking. Soon it was time to return for afternoon Sunday school. After a short break for tea, the older family members hurried back for the evening service. Remembering his early church life John spoke of sitting on the hard pew during long services and how much of an endurance test this was for an active young boy. Yet this, and all the disciplines of life in a large family, were used by God to mould him into a soldier of Jesus Christ.

Any activity or pursuit that was considered secular was discouraged on Sundays. Reading material had to be the Bible or missionary books. The children who were not old enough to attend the evening service gathered round the piano to sing hymns, with Rose as the pianist. Afterwards she would read missionary books to them. Some were very exciting, with hair-raising stories of the work of pioneer missionaries among ferocious tribes and cannibals. These men and women had left home with only one vision – to spend their lives reaching the unreached for Christ, whatever the cost. Often that cost involved giving up their lives for the sake of the Gospel. John was, therefore, introduced to the idea of mission early in life. His aunt, Evie Brand, was a missionary with the Strict Baptist Mission in India and his sisters Ruth and Monica later also went to India with the SBM.

Towards the end of his life, John spoke of his early spiritual journey.

> As a very small child the Lord caused me to believe, and as a schoolboy He showed me that He *wanted* me and would 'see of the travail of His soul and be satisfied' by my coming to Him, my deliverer.

He was baptized at the age of twelve in Mount Zion Strict Baptist Church.

John was an active, talkative boy. He was known in the family as the chatterbox, and someone once suggested that he had been vaccinated with a gramophone needle! He certainly had his mischievous moments. Ruth remembers him scraping a hole in the nursery wall and talking to an imaginary friend for long periods. On one occasion he went missing for a long time and, in spite of searching, no one could find him. Anxiety was relieved when the narrow coat cupboard in the nursery was opened and there he was, standing straight as a ramrod. What had motivated him to do this no one ever knew.

Bertie Harris felt that John would benefit from the companionship of other boys, since he had been surrounded mainly by sisters. As boarding school was considered by some to be a good preparation for life John was sent, aged seven, to a preparatory school in Bexhill. At first this was a very difficult experience for a young boy from such a close and sheltered family. He was small for his age, and bullying at the school sometimes amounted to cruelty. John once told a sister that there were older boys who knocked nails into the knees of the young and defenceless ones. However, his experiences on moving to Monkton Combe Junior School in Bath, and on into the senior school, were much more positive. He came to appreciate the quality of education offered, especially as it prepared him to use his linguistic gift to learn five different languages in the three countries in which he later worked.

Bertie had a wholesale grocery business, which he had taken over from his father. No doubt he would have been pleased if a son had followed in his footsteps, but this was not to be. One day John's cousin, Paul Brand, who was a medical student, came to number 18 to play tennis with the older members of the family. Paul told John that if he could sit still long enough he would teach him about the anatomy of the hand. Even as a student Paul's absorption with the hand, later to make his surgery famous in the field of leprosy, kept the ten-year-old John engrossed. He had glimpsed something of the fearful and wonderful work of God.

Paul's fascination influenced John, and from school he went on to study medicine at St Bartholomew's Hospital in London. His early years of training included a time studying in Cambridge, where medical students were sent during the war.

It was during his medical training that John went through a 'dark tunnel' of spiritual experience. He continued his reading of Scripture and memorized many passages, but he lacked the joy of the Lord and felt bound by legalism. He was to find release through the ministry of Tom Gray, and fellowship among friends in the London City Mission (LCM) Hall in South Ealing. He first visited the hall with others from the youth group of Mount Zion Church for an evening with the young people of the Mission. It was during that evening, or soon afterwards, that God met with John and he entered into a new, deeper and more joyful relationship with Him. Such joy in the Lord and whole-hearted devotion to Him characterized John's life from then on. The Mission and the home of Tom and Mary Gray became his spiritual places of refreshment. He soon became a Sunday school teacher at the Mission and was eager to take part in as many church activities as possible, especially door-to-door visiting. He also enjoyed joining the London City missionaries on Friday evenings at Speakers' Corner in Hyde Park, on his way home from his studies. It was there in Hyde Park, on one of those Friday evenings in September 1948, that a special and lasting friendship was formed.

Peter Dahlen, the son of a Swedish consul to Australia, had recently finished his national service, spent minesweeping around Australian coasts, and had then come to the UK intending to study English literature at Oxford University. Of this period of his life he later wrote, 'I was desperate to know the Lord.' He came to London to see the sights, and one of the places mentioned in his guide book was Speakers' Corner. One Friday evening he headed for Hyde Park. Tom Gray was explaining the Gospel with great clarity to a group of passers-by. John was helping there too, after his day's work at Bart's Hospital. He approached Peter and asked if he was interested in what he had heard. He certainly was, so John took him across to Tom. After walking around the park talking with his new friends Peter was led to the Lord. God had prepared his heart to accept the message of salvation.

After that day in Hyde Park a friendship of great spiritual depth grew between John and Peter. John inspired Peter, who, as a young Christian, was keen to share in his experience and rejoice in his newly found relationship with the Lord. Peter later wrote down some memories of those days.

> We spent much time together. On all these occasions our friendship was based on our fellowship with the Lord. John's knowledge of Scripture was of such value to me as we shared together. I remember going on a car journey with him. As he drove he quoted to me from an Epistle. I sat there with an open Bible to correct where necessary. His aim was to learn complete Epistles by heart. We spent time in prayer, which was so important and real to him. His intercessory ministry was unique. We also went out visiting in the district together and took part in open-air

meetings with the LCM. We went to missionary meetings, both of us seeking to know God's will. I will always
remember when God clarified to him that he was to go to
Belgian Congo with WEC [Worldwide Evangelisation
Crusade], and he was given the verse from Isaiah 44:3, 'For
I will pour water on the thirsty land, and streams on the
dry ground; I will pour out my Spirit on your offspring,
and my blessing on your descendents.' He held on to this
until he actually saw the fulfilment in revival in Belgian
Congo. John was a person who took God seriously and
therefore enjoyed God immensely.

Mary Gray recalled the weeks following Peter's conversion.
There were some incidents that remained clearly etched on
her memory.

Peter also joined in door-to-door visiting, not only around
the Mission but across the main road to a council estate. At
first the children were brought across to the Mission but
then it seemed best to hire the local school hall for Sunday
afternoons. Does this make door-to-door visiting sound
easy? No, everybody did not come, but nearly everybody
did hear about Jesus. There were some unexpected deter-
rents to reaching people in their homes. It was either John
who had an aversion to dogs, or the dogs that had an aversion to him. During their visit to one street John unlatched
the gate of number 16 and found himself confronted with
two large and angry dogs, barking and growling and
throwing their weight against the fence. He quickly re-
treated, and when meeting up with Tom and Peter re-

marked, 'I really feel led to suggest you two visit number 16 next time.'

There was also a time when Mary had cause to be thankful for John's willingness to help in a practical way.

> Even before he qualified, John made use of his medical knowledge to help where he could. Health care in those days was not so easily available and there was no ready access to antibiotics or inoculations against a whole range of virulent diseases. Health care for mothers after their babies were born was only just being thought about. It was John who noticed that I needed help after the birth of my fourth baby, a happy boy who had tipped the scales at eleven and a quarter pounds. Seeing my need for hospital care, John took the baby under his wing for a few hours until a friend from the Mission was found to take over during my six weeks in hospital.

However, John's newly discovered spiritual freedom was misunderstood within his family and resulted in alienation from his father. From Bertie's point of view there were probably two main causes for hurt. One was his son leaving Mount Zion Strict Baptist Church and finding his spiritual home elsewhere. Loyalty to the family's church was considered to be of major importance. Then there was the step that John took of being baptized again, as a testimony to the renewal of his spiritual life. The severed relationship caused pain in the family for a while. Thankfully, the rift was healed later and in 1950 father and son enjoyed a time of special fellowship when John visited Bertie in hospital as he was recovering after an operation. Bertie gave John the blessing found in Numbers 6:24–6:

> The Lord bless thee and keep thee,
> the Lord make His face shine upon thee, and be gracious unto thee,
> the Lord lift up his countenance upon thee, and give thee peace.'   (KJV)

On the day following John's visit, Bertie died suddenly and unexpectedly of a pulmonary embolism. John, on his seventieth birthday, bestowed the same blessing upon the three generations of his family that were present.

2

Preparation and Partings

After qualifying in 1949 John went to Mildmay Mission Hospital, in London's Bethnal Green district, to spend two weeks as a locum. Until it was taken over by the NHS this Christian hospital was supported by donations. Even today it relies heavily on prayer and charitable gifts to help maintain its high standard of care. When John arrived at the hospital he found that though it was austere, a family atmosphere prevailed. The staff demonstrated the love of Christ, and this had a big impact on the local community.

Many of the doctors and nurses working there were in training for overseas missionary service, and it proved a tough time of preparation. Yet in spite of staff shortages and long duty hours wonderful lifelong friendships were formed, which compensated for the hardness endured. Nora Vickers, who was training at Mildmay, remembers John's first meeting with nurse Elsie Sexstone.

> The very serious young junior doctor was the last person we would have suspected of having noticed us nurses. But we began to realize that he *had* noticed Elsie.

The Lord showed John that Elsie was to be his wife. At first Elsie did not respond to his interest in her. She wanted to keep her eyes focused on her clear call to serve the Lord overseas, with no emotional relationships to divert her. But John was not easily put off. When he was convinced that a certain course was the will of God he persevered, despite delays and setbacks, to see it accomplished. He returned to his work at Bart's Hospital, waiting and praying for God's answer. This came when Elsie also heard God speak, assuring her that John was to be her life partner. From this time on their friendship blossomed into true love.

John and Elsie were both Londoners, but from opposite ends of the city, as Elsie was born in Greenwich. Like John, she was a child of her parents' second marriages. Some of the children from their first marriages had already left home by the time Elsie was born, but they visited from time to time. The youngest child, she was brought up with two older brothers. Her father worked for London Transport. Money was not plentiful, but there was enough to live on, and Elsie remembers deriving much pleasure from the simple things in life as a child. However, she saw many signs of distress among unemployed neighbours around them. Extreme poverty, drink and disease devastated homes. Tuberculosis, diphtheria and scarlet fever were major killers. Leslie, one of Elsie's older brothers, contracted tuberculosis and only recovered thanks to his mother's skilful care.

Local activity centred around three places: the small general store, the public house and the mission hall. Most things could be purchased at the store, where neighbourhood news was also on offer. Many local people spent more time than was good for them in the public house. The mission hall made people aware of overseas mission from Sunday school onwards, and it was here that Elsie learned of the Lord's Great Commission of Matthew 28:19. She later taught in the Sunday school herself with one of her older sisters, Grace, who continued serving there for over forty years. The area has now radically changed. The public house and shop are no longer there, but the mission hall remains.

The war brought drastic changes to Elsie's family life. Aged twelve, she was sent to Sussex as an evacuee. She would be sixteen before she could return to London. For the first three years away she was placed in a home that was not very welcoming to children. Meanwhile, her parents were facing the bombing raids and all the traumas of living in wartime London and, knowing this, she was unwilling to burden them with her problems. So, as a young believer, she learned to bring her unhappiness to the Lord and to know His help. The experience strengthened her spiritual life. For her last year as an evacuee she was placed with a lovely Christian couple and saw for herself a Christian home in action. After finishing school, Elsie returned to London to work in an office.

The horrors of the air raids were all around her, and one of her school friends was killed. Her own office was bombed on a Sunday, so the staff escaped injury. She was once on a packed train when the station it had just left was demolished by a rocket. On another occasion her life was spared when a doodlebug exploded near to where she had thrown herself to the ground. It was so close that she remembers seeing the swastika on its side as it sped towards her. A nearby row of houses was demolished. God's angels were certainly protecting His child for the assignment He had planned for her.

Since her days at the mission hall in Greenwich Elsie's call to go and serve the Lord overseas had become increasingly clear. After four years in secretarial work the way opened up for her to train as a nurse at Mildmay Mission Hospital, and this significant step in her life brought her into contact with John. They got engaged in 1950. After attending a number of mission meetings together, their attention was drawn towards leprosy sufferers in Belgian Congo (the territory renamed Zaire in 1971 and since 1997 known as the Democratic Republic of the Congo). This led to their sending applications to train as missionaries with WEC.

Both John and Elsie were accepted by WEC and they entered into what was to be a long period of preparation. John was sent to Antwerp for a three-month intensive tropical medicine course, in French. This was followed by a rigorous character building course, known as WEC Orientation, which lasted for six months. Candidates cleaned windows, helped in the kitchens and learned to undertake willingly any task assigned to them. There were extended times of prayer and learning about different areas of missionary service. It was during this time that God taught John to rely on Him in the area of finance.

> As a candidate in a faith mission, I had no experience of living by faith for finance. I was concerned about this, and one day asked the Lord that if He wanted me to give away my small savings and prove Him in prayer for finance, He would let me receive that very day a certain amount I

needed. No one had given me money except for Christmas or birthdays, so it was a tall order. Later that day a Congo missionary came towards me waving a bank note. His face was radiant and he said, 'Tithe money, John.' It was the exact amount I had asked for. I am still learning with great joy that it is more blessed to give than to receive.

Looking back many years later on this incident, and many other experiences of answered prayer over the years, John summed up his own conviction.

Someone has said, 'the right kind of prayer is the most potent instrumentality known on earth.' I have proved it.

Elsie began a two-year Bible training course at Mount Hermon Missionary Training College in Ealing. At every stage students had to find the finance to support them, and for Elsie this meant taking jobs in the college vacations, sometimes as a district nurse and sometimes as a secretary. Separation from John at such an early stage in their relationship was a trial for them both. Elsie soon realized that John would be ready to leave for Africa long before her. Completing all that was required of her, in training and preparation, seemed like a huge and challenging mountain ahead of her. Climbing the huge mountain meant a six-year-long engagement, but she doggedly persevered, one step at a time. Her older sister, Grace, after becoming a Christian herself, had introduced the young Elsie to the Lord. Now Grace gave her wonderful, prayerful support. The other members of her family looked on with incredulity.

John's call to undertake leprosy work in Belgian Congo came about initially through reading a book about the life of the missionary Edith Moules, written by an author named Norman Grubb. His calling was confirmed by the Lord in an unmistakable way. In the early 1940s WEC missionaries Robert and Ivy Milliken started a work in a village called Malingwia, in north-east Belgian Congo. It wasn't long before a church was established. The Pastor (named Mattiasi) had parents with leprosy, therefore he was concerned to reach the many people in the area suffering from this disease. At a conference in 1945 the African Church requested that WEC build a leprosarium in Malingwia. With Government permission, this was initiated.

An area of forest was cleared and huts were built. A young couple, Arthur and Irene Scott (a nurse), offered to come and be involved. Soon the leprosy sufferers were installed and the work established. In 1950 the church committee made a request to the missionaries for a doctor to help with the project. The missionaries replied that they saw no harm in writing to ask if this was possible. Soon afterwards a letter detailing the need for a doctor arrived at the WEC headquarters in Upper Norwood, London, and was placed on the desk of Norman Grubb, now a WEC leader. He read it while dealing with the business of the day. His work was interrupted by a young doctor, John Harris, being shown into his office. Having been in touch with WEC concerning overseas service, John had come to say that he felt God was calling him to leprosy work in Belgian Congo. Norman Grubb showed him the letter he had received that morning. This surely was a sign of God's call, and John gave Him the glory.

Elsie joined a group of WEC friends at Liverpool Street station to say goodbye to her fiancé. It was spring 1953, and John was leaving with other missionaries to board a ship called the *Dunottar Castle*, which would take them the five thousand miles to Mombasa in Kenya. There on the platform, after the singing of hymns and offering of prayers, came the goodbyes. As Elsie watched the train moving away, with John waving from the window, her heart was full and heavy. She had no idea when they would be together again.

It was a time of severe testing for them both. Elsie had learned something of separation when she had been parted from her family during the war. Many more partings were to come. Only as both she and John agreed to move in obedience to the Lord's guidance did the painful separations become possible to bear.

3

Proving the Power of Prayer

After three weeks at sea, John arrived at the bustling port of Mombasa. The African continent, so often the scene of suffering and turmoil, was now witnessing the horrific Mau Mau terrorist uprising, which aimed to expel all European settlers and end British rule in Kenya. John was made very aware of the conflict as he began his first journey into Africa. He was taken across Kenya and Uganda and eventually arrived at the border with Belgian Congo, after travelling some distance by river boat. Veteran missionary Jim Grainger met him at the border with an old vehicle, which had seen better days. Together they travelled the long and rough road to the WEC mission headquarters in Ibambi, in the north-east. At one stage the old truck slid off a bridge and landed in a river. No one was hurt, but there was a frustrating delay as the vehicle was hauled on to dry land.

All the hazards of the long journey were forgotten on arrival in Ibambi, where the welcome John received was overwhelming. No knowledge of the local language was needed to see what God was doing after years of spiritual dryness. Blessing was flowing into people's lives like cascades of living water. After a short time of orientation John was assigned to the mission centre in Malingwia, the most northerly of WEC's centres in Belgian Congo. He stayed with Robert and Ivy Milliken and immediately made learning the Bangala language a priority. His hosts agreed to help him by speaking only Bangala in their home. (Though their young son, Robert, understood English, he had to learn to speak it at the age of four when on UK furlough.) John also gained his knowledge of Bangala by going out among the local people, communicating with them and helping to alleviate their medical needs. He acquired a bicycle and cycled daily the one mile to the leprosarium, locally called the 'camp'. One could imagine him using these journeys to go over his Bangala phrases. He always made it his practice to memorize Scripture verses whenever he learned a new language.

According to a Government ruling in the 1950s, leprosy sufferers had to be segregated from their fellow villagers. Being permanently separated from family members caused sadness. Yet each sufferer built their own hut with the help of others, and each had a small plot for growing vegetables and for cultivating a cash crop of either coffee or cotton. Local Christians gave up land for the camp, and the patients gladly shared the produce of the land with the believers.

At this time, the more modern drugs that could slow down and sometimes even cure leprosy were unknown in this area. Ulceration of hands and feet was a baffling problem, and many patients were badly deformed. John did what he could to alleviate their suffering. He also treated many other medical conditions that he had not encountered in London, such as malaria, filaria and an innumerable variety of worms.

Belgian Congo/Zaire

His surgical skills were soon put to the test when it became clear that a local woman about to give birth needed a Caesarean section. John admitted that he had never performed this operation before, having only observed others. Some of his non-medical colleagues – Delores Meyers, an American teacher, and the Millikens – bravely offered to assist. No expert help was available. John asked for prayer support from all those involved, inviting the local Christians and schoolchildren to pray as well. It was always his custom to pray with his patient and those assisting in operations – before giving himself wholeheartedly to the job in hand, he had to have first sought the Lord's help. The operation was successfully performed, resulting in a healthy child and a happy mother.

Another medical challenge came when he was called upon to remove a growth on an eye. The patient was a Portuguese owner of a coffee plantation. He was so grateful for his treatment that he donated an old truck. Since Robert Milliken was a real jack of all trades he dismantled the truck to take advantage of the working parts. Using the front wheels, steering and suspension, he somehow managed to make two adjustable operating tables – one for the camp and one for the community hospital.

Robert Milliken, a few months before he went to be with his Lord, recorded John's early days in Malingwia.

> Although John could not as yet hear all that was going on in Bangala, we could see that he understood in his spirit what was taking place and he entered into it all with us. He was in his element with all that God was doing in sending revival. Lives were being changed among the Christians and people everywhere were being converted. We could see that John loved times of prayer together with Africans and missionaries. He took a deep interest in the work of others around him. As he joined in prayer times with the missionaries they were amazed how he prayed in detail for all the practical work of the station, not concentrating only on his own side of the work. Everyone, he used to say,

should uphold each other in every aspect of work which has to be done. So encouragement was given all round.

Elsie battled on with her preparation to join John. Malingwia had no radio or telephone contact and no missionary planes to provide a regular link with the outside world, but however long John's letters took to arrive, Elsie looked forward to them eagerly. They always provided a spiritual feast. The huge mountain was gradually being scaled as she spent time learning French in Switzerland, completed a practical tropical diseases course for nurses in Liverpool and, in between, helped in the kitchen at the WEC headquarters in London. She had many opportunities to exercise trust in the Lord. She once needed £100 to enable her to get to her studies in Switzerland, but she only had a few shillings at the time. On a visit to her wartime evacuation home, she was having her shoes mended in a shop run by one of the family members. Without any knowledge of her financial situation, he suddenly said, 'Do you need £100? The Lord keeps telling me you do.' Elsie gave thanks for this wonderful answer to her prayers and set off for Switzerland. During her study of tropical diseases she was responsible for looking after a leprosy patient. She was being prepared for her future with John.

In March 1955 Elsie was again on Liverpool Street station, only this time she was the one leaning out of the window as the train drew out. Saying goodbye to her close family was hard, but at last she was going to Africa to begin the work that God had prepared for her and John.

Elsie's five-week long journey from Liverpool Street to Ibambi was even more eventful than John's. There were ample opportunities to experience God protecting her life. A terrific storm blew up in the Mediterranean Sea as the ship neared Marseilles. She felt terribly alone, homesick and seasick. Then came news that a lifeboat and all its crew had been lost while trying to rescue a fishing boat, which had suffered the same fate. But there were brighter moments. Later in the voyage, two welcome visitors came aboard to cheer her up. The first was Peter Dahlen, who was now working with the Red Sea Mission team in Aden. Sailing out to the ship in a small boat, he brought encouragement and fellowship. The second, unexpected, visitor boarded the *Dunottar Castle* when it docked at Port Said. A lady carrying a bunch of roses came on board and greeted Elsie. She turned out to be a missionary, named Cicely Radley, who had worked for many years in Egypt as a teacher. In fact, she was the first missionary Elsie had ever heard about, and she had prayed for her as a child in Sunday school.

Disembarking at Mombasa turned out to be a nightmare, as there was a dock strike in progress. The luggage was unloaded, some of it landing in the water and floating across to the dockside. After that it was every man for himself as passengers battled to find their possessions. Elsie got separated from her travelling companions in the chaos. She could see some of her trunks and, horror of horrors, some of the locks were broken. There was no way she could retrieve them by herself. Although people all around her were shouting, she felt so alone. In her panic and weakness she prayed, 'Please Lord, send an angel to deliver me.'

Almost immediately, a hand was placed on her shoulder and a voice asked, 'Do you need help?' She turned, and seeing a man standing there, said impulsively, 'You look like a very substantial angel!' After she explained, he said he was from an agricultural mission in Kenya and had come to the docks to meet a new candidate. Having met, they had started to leave. Suddenly, he had felt prompted to return to the luggage shed to help someone in need. The man retrieved Elsie's luggage, found some wire to make it safe and then asked an official to seal the trunks for the onward journey. Travelling on by train and river boat through Kenya, Elsie watched as the luggage was hurled around and felt profoundly thankful for the dockside stranger God had sent.

The journey from the border to Ibambi included various enforced stops. The vehicle was even less roadworthy than when it had transported John in 1953. One stop, at the small centre of Nyankunde, took on special significance for Elsie, linking both the past and the future. An American couple, Mr and Mrs Deans, had set up a printing press here. They served with the Brethren Mission among several different tribes. Elsie had first heard of them as an evacuee in Sussex. Her wartime carers had prayed for this missionary couple in Africa, and Elsie had joined in. Now she was actually meeting them and seeing the answers to their prayers. 'What a lovely rosy complexion you have,' said Mrs Deans, adding, 'but not for long in this climate!' The comment sounded rather ominous to Elsie at the time. In the 1960s, various missions united to build a large medical centre at Nyankunde. John and Elsie would later live here for seventeen years until John's death in 1995.

Lifted from her seat in the back of the truck and carried around, shoulder-high, among singing crowds, Elsie was engulfed by the welcome. She had arrived in Ibambi! Her arrival was celebrated with home-made banners and great rejoicing. But where was John? WEC, like many other missionary organizations in this era, had very strict rules for missionaries, especially relating to engagement and marriage. John was many kilometres away in Malingwia. Although to modern readers these restrictions may seem unfeeling, they were accepted then as part of the calling. God's work must come first. Preparation for service must be completed before affairs of the heart were given a place. Commitment meant discipline in every area of life. John and Elsie soon found out it was not easy. They were so near now, but it was to be ten months before they were married.

Elsie was looked after by the Field Leader and his wife, Mr and Mrs Scholes. During her six weeks' orientation she shared a house with Dr Helen Roseveare, who had a small dispensary and who was working on a simple teaching textbook. Elsie typed for her in Swahili, and then, in the afternoons, she learned the Bangala language for an hour. Not long before the end of her six weeks, Mr Scholes asked her to come for a chat. She was dumbfounded to discover that her first assignment was to take over the teaching at a boarding school for about two hundred boys. She would move to Nala, a small WEC station, and two untrained national teachers would take care of the first grades. Evidently, the lady who ran the school was seriously ill and the replacement teacher was still completing the mandatory teacher training in Belgium. Mr Scholes must have seen her look of shock. She was a nurse and midwife, and had no experience of teaching. As if to compensate for his shattering news, he mentioned that he had to make a weekend visit to Malingwia. Would she like to accompany him?

At last she would see John after their separation of two years. She set off with Mr Scholes over the rough road in the same old vehicle. It finally broke down within seven kilometres of Malingwia. Mr Scholes sent a messenger to ask Robert Milliken to bring a towing vehicle to meet them. Then they sat by the roadside and waited in the hot sun. It was a relief when a moving speck appeared in the distance and they realized it was a motorcycle roaring towards them. Just visible in a cloud of dust, there was John, riding pillion. It was hardly the romantic reunion Elsie had hoped for, but they were together. However, much had to remain unsaid, and the weekend was soon over. Custom and decorum meant they always had to meet in the company of others. Elsie's emotions were in turmoil as she returned with Mr Scholes to Ibambi. She wondered when she would see John again. At least she had seen Malingwia, where they would start their married life. But her heart was trembling with fear at the thought of what lay ahead of her at the school.

On her first day all the pupils assembled for prayers. As Elsie called the register, she tried to pronounce names unintelligible to her. Ripples of laughter spread through the assembly and she felt like running away. But in a flash of inspiration, she started to laugh with them. From that moment she felt at home and accepted among the boys.

Her six months or so at the school, with so many new experiences, taught her to rely more on the Lord for His help. While feeling desperately inadequate, she found she was able to do things she never thought possible. The place seemed riddled with snakes, but she learned to cope with them. However, the longed-for letters from John often took longer to arrive than when she had been receiving mail from him in the UK!

★　★　★　★　★

At last the day came when the Field Leader arrived to say that she and John could begin to prepare papers for their marriage. When these were in order, a date could be set. Belgian administration was very meticulous, and there was much filling in of forms to be done. In January 1956 Elsie left Nala to return to Malingwia and prepare for her marriage to John.

The couple were granted an hour each day in which to be together. Finally they had some time to talk and pray about so many things. Their wedding was the first marriage of missionaries to take place in Malingwia, and there was much to plan. When relatives at home heard of one decision they reached, they were perplexed. Even some missionaries found it puzzling. Elsie had brought out a white wedding dress, made especially for her. But, sensitive to the revival blessing and simple local custom, John wanted to minimize outward show and possible distraction. Their wedding was to emphasize their union in the Lord, and, to John, the dress would be inappropriate. Elsie, no different from most wives in treasuring their wedding gown, showed

Christlike humility when John explained how he felt. She understood, and agreed not to wear the dress.

Things did not quite run to plan! A civil wedding had been scheduled to take place on the 18th January in Buta, fifty kilometres away, with the church wedding on the 19th. On arrival at the Government offices at Buta, John and Elsie's papers were scrutinized and one was found to be missing. Regulations had to be obeyed, so they returned to Malingwia and the church wedding had to be moved to the 21st. On the 20th, the missing paper was brought to Malingwia by the Field Leader, so they were able to set off once more for Buta. They arrived safely, feeling rather hot and dusty after the journey. There seemed to be nowhere they could go to refresh themselves. To their immense relief, all the papers were found to be in order. They waited for an hour in a nearby park while the Belgian official disappeared to don his white suit, which had to be worn for such an occasion. Looking immaculate, he conducted the ceremony with solemnity. The table where he was seated was covered with a green cloth and decorated with tiny white flowers. In response to his rapid French, John and Elsie said 'oui' at the required moments. Shaking hands with the couple at the close of the cermony, the official presented Elsie with a '*livret du marriage*' with places in it for the names of fourteen children. John and Elsie returned to Malingwia tired, but relieved that the first part of their marriage had been accomplished. Before going to bed, Elsie took John's suit out of his trunk, where it had been for over two years, and pressed it with a charcoal-fired iron.

Calendars indicated the 21st January 1956. The church wedding day had dawned. Elsie was awakened early by a knock at the door. A voice said, 'Elsie are you up? We've got work to do.' It was John. He explained that the local chief had sent for a list of all the three hundred leprosy patients in the camp. He needed it immediately. From 6 a.m. to 8 a.m. John dictated their names, while Elsie frantically kept up with him on her typewriter. Elsie gently reminded him that this was their wedding day. He smiled and the work went on. This was Africa, where surprises crop up at every turn. After a quick breakfast, John did his usual round of the wards and found a young boy needing a hernia operation. Elsie got busy cleaning the operating theatre, then prepared all the instruments. At this point it was found that an operation was not needed after all. By the time they left the hospital the guests had already gathered in the church for the wedding, and had started singing. The couple had to hurry to their homes to get changed quickly – Elsie into a simple blue dress with white hat, shoes and gloves and John into his beautifully ironed suit. Together they entered the church, which had been tastefully decorated, and the large congregation stood up and sang a welcome with their arms upraised. Elsie was handed a bouquet of local flowers arranged by one of the missionaries. After more songs of praise and prayer, a talk in Bangala on Psalm 45 was given by Mr Scholes. The newlyweds left the church to find that the men had formed a guard of honour, with Bibles raised to form an arch. Elsie remembers John holding her arm so tightly that she had to whisper to him, 'I won't run away, there's nowhere to go!' As they arrived at the reception, the house helpers presented them with an enormous flower arrangement. The home-made wedding cake was flanked by two sponges prepared by Mrs Scholes. On one she had written, 'Jesus Himself drew near,' and on the other, 'and went with them'. After a much needed rest, a simple English ceremony was held in the home of a missionary. There was a moment of panic as John searched for the ring. A missionary was heard to remark, 'He badly needs a wife!' Marriage vows were exchanged, and John put the ring on Elsie's finger. They were now, at last, well and truly man and wife.

John and Elsie's wedding day

4

A New Assignment

There were no plans for a honeymoon. John and Elsie set up their new home in a small, round house, originally built for a single person. On the Monday following the wedding, Elsie was at her husband's side assisting in an operation. Elsie found that John already had the confidence of the local people, but she, as a new arrival, was still being tried out. Her new life demanded a great many adjustments. She had to cope with a house helper who was most unhelpful. He was an elderly man who always seemed to be grumpy. Since there was no running water, every drop had to be carried up a long slope. She had no fridge, and before bread could be made the weevils had to be picked out of the flour. When cooking, she battled with either the smell of smoke from the wood stove or the taste of kerosene from the oil burner in the food. She taught five to ten-year-olds the three Rs in their mud-thatch school, while somehow fitting in her own language learning and medical work. It was all so different from her life at the school in Nala. John was very occupied, as he had begun training local people as nurses, but he understood Elsie's struggle to adapt. His enthusiasm cheered her on and they shared their joy at being together at last. Every day, one or the other would cycle to see the leprosy patients at the camp, but soon Elsie had to give up the bicycle for a time. She was expecting their first baby.

Just before David was born they moved from the round house to a small dwelling with the added benefit of a galvanized roof. Pat Holdaway was asked to be at hand to assist in the delivery of the baby. Pat, a nurse from New Zealand, was in her first term as part of the WEC team in Malingwia and lived in the house that had been vacated by John and Elsie. She was efficient and full of eagerness to serve the Lord. The week before Elsie's expected time for delivery she had gone for a teaching weekend in a village a few kilometres away. Her journey back to Malingwia was delayed because of a collapsed bridge. When she eventually arrived, David had made it first, helped into the world by his father. Pat was a great help to Elsie in caring for David, especially as she was not able to feed him herself. Feeds had to be prepared with powdered milk. When John was around, he willingly undertook this job for his son.

David had been born on the 25th October 1956. The following January, the missionaries working in the vast north-east area, sixty in all, including children, gathered in Ibambi for the WEC Field Conference. It meant a journey of three hundred kilometres for John and his family. They were accommodated in student housing and soon discovered that it was infested with mosquitoes. David did not escape being bitten and, just before the end of the conference, Elsie realized their three-month-old baby had malaria. This was a serious illness for a young child. Helen Roseveare, who was responsible for his treatment, saw that little David was not responding and warned his parents one evening that he was unlikely to survive the night. On hearing this serious prognosis, John and Elsie spent time in prayer for David as his life ebbed away. While praying, they were guided to inject subcutaneous fluids at intervals into his tiny body, as his greatest need was fluid replacement. Intravenous fluids by drip were not available at the time. He was also given injections of quinine. Evidence of God's healing power was shown as David gradually responded. John and Elsie were full of praise to the Lord for sparing their son, who soon returned to his normal, healthy self. Many years later John wrote of David's healing, 'Certainly it is not always the Lord's will to heal. However, our son's recovery was an unspeakable encouragement.'

At the conference, John and Elsie were given a new assignment. In a few months they would be transferred from Malingwia to WEC's medical centre in Nebobongo, just seven kilometres from Ibambi. They would be working with Helen Roseveare, who had been in Belgian Congo for four years and who urgently needed the help of another doctor in her expanding medical programme. The village was in a strategic position for a medical centre with two doctors. There was good access by road from the north and the south, giving opportunity for desperately needy people to reach specialized medical and surgical aid. Local Christians supported this new vision.

Learning Swahili, the trade language used in Nebobongo, became the next challenge for John. He set aside a week for study, as always preparing words and phrases to enable him to communicate with the local people on arrival. Elsie had her hands full at the new centre,

David being now seven months old, but she found that she could use her knowledge of Bangala effectively among local people.

Helen Roseveare took up the story.

> I had been in Belgian Congo for about three months when John and Elsie arrived, and it was with a tremendous sense of relief that I welcomed them. There were now two doctors in the WEC team. I was no longer the only one. However, for the first three or four years we worked about four hundred miles apart, separated by appallingly bad roads. Then John was appointed by the Field Committee in 1957 to come to join me at Nebobongo, ostensibly, at the time, to train me in surgery, so that I might go to the far south of our region to open a new medical work there.
>
> I remember getting the big house ready to welcome them. We repainted all the walls, adding chemical dyes to the whitewash, a different colour for each room: red permanganate in one, yellow flavine in another, malachite green in a third and methylene blue in the fourth. So far so good. We expected them on a certain Thursday, and we killed a chicken and got everything ready to welcome them for lunch. The truck failed to make it. This was repeated for three successive weeks. On the fifth week we had no more chickens, and they arrived! But even the absence of a good meal could not dampen the welcome, the only sad thing being that all the chemical dyes in the whitewash had blanched in the bright sunshine, and no one knew there was any difference in the four rooms unless they looked behind a picture!

John was amazingly patient with me. His medical knowledge and expertise were far superior to mine; I had muddled through for four years, but I was not a competent clinician. John began to tidy things up, and the medical care of patients and the training of students definitely began to improve.

Looking back Elsie remembers some of the medical emergencies that they faced at this time.

One day a young man came screaming through the compound with a gangrenous arm, with flies swarming around it. He had come from a forest area and must have travelled for a long time in this condition. He was an untreated epileptic and thought to be mad by his fellow Africans. In a fit he had fallen into the fire and this was the result. The arm had to be amputated quickly, which John did with Helen assisting, and I gave the anaesthetic. The severed arm was solemnly buried in a hole with the relatives watching. As he recovered he was treated for epilepsy and was able to lead a reasonably normal life.

Another evening a man arrived at the front door just before dusk announcing there had been a fight. After considerable delay in coming to the point he eventually made us to understand that someone had been hurt in the fighting. He pointed to a woman standing there who then pulled back her cloth to reveal an enormous abdominal knife wound. She had walked quite a long distance from her village to Nebobongo after the incident and was standing there during all the preliminary talking. This was an example of the endurance we saw many times in the

> sufferings of our African friends. It took a long time to
> stitch her up.

So life for John and Elsie was often exciting, sometimes
daunting and always demanding. They appreciated having
Helen as a co-worker. There were so many serious medical
cases, obstetric problems and desperately sick babies. Many
patients arrived at the medical centre in a bad condition,
due to the way in which practitioners of witchcraft had
tried to heal them. Elsie took on the responsibility of looking after the midwifery unit and teaching the midwifery
students. The students came from various areas and had
been selected by the church, but many were far too young
and immature to be in such work. Some had only just left
school, and as they were from different tribes, spoke different languages and ate different food, it was hard for them to
work together as a team. Elsie was helped by a lady known
as Mama Damaris. In the past Mama Damaris had led a life
of sin, but the Lord had met with her during a time of
revival and she came to the work as His joyful, peaceful servant. She not only took over the supervision of the student
nurses, but also worked in the maternity unit and managed,
after being taught by Helen and Elsie, to pass a Red Cross
exam. God was preparing her for the time when all expatriates would have to leave Nebobongo and she would be left
in charge.

The work of the team in Nebobongo touched people in
need of medical and surgical care, with Helen mainly dealing with the former and John the latter. Elsie valiantly tried
to accommodate both doctors. Her burden was eased when

another nurse, Florence Stebbing, arrived back from furlough to strengthen the team. Florence had worked with Helen before and was a cheerful, hard-working person. She recalled the time of her arrival and settling in Nebobongo.

> Both Elsie and John were most kind to me. They took me under their care and taught me what I needed to know, especially as it was to be my job to make up the daily medicines for patients. Also, the way they cared for their patients taught me much. John was always kind and courteous and willing to help if he could. I was sorry when they moved on.

* * * * *

During this time of caring for patients with many different illnesses, John had not forgotten his main calling – that he should work with leprosy sufferers. As there was also a leprosy settlement in Nebobongo, John and Elsie took to their bicycles to visit. The pioneer missionary, Edith Moules, who had founded this settlement in 1940, had planted many chaulmoogra trees. The oil from these trees was injected into the skin of leprosy patients. Although it was said to have medicinal qualities for leprosy, in fact it was of doubtful benefit and left many scars where it had been administered. As in Malingwia, the patients suffered segregation, deformity (especially of hands), and sores where their insensitive skin had been damaged by trauma caused by burns and pressure. They could not feel when damage was inflicted. But John and Elsie found that many had a true and radiant faith in the Lord. Attending their worship times was an inspiration.

John had read of the surgical reconstruction operations his cousin Paul Brand was performing in India. There were many under John's care whom he felt would benefit greatly from such surgical procedures. There always has to be a first in any new venture, and John operated on a widow who had suffered from leprosy for many years. Her job entailed caring for a group of children, and like many African women she had the task of drawing water and carrying the bucket home. However, she had a dropped wrist, which prevented her from holding a bucket of water. Using the techniques developed by Paul Brand, John was able to fix her wrist into a position that enabled her to carry water. This brought joy to both her and her surgeon!

The team in Nebobongo was depleted when Helen went on an extended furlough in order to do more training. When John and Elsie were finally able to prepare for home leave in 1960 they were very much in need of a break! John had been in Africa for seven and a half years and Elsie for five and a half. By this time Lois Grace had joined the family, born on the 15th October 1959. Once again, John had been involved in the delivery, this time with Florence Stebbing in attendance.

But storm clouds were gathering. The time for Congolese independence from Belgium was drawing near, and years of turmoil were to follow. Belgian Congo (originally named Congo Free State from 1885–1908) had been established in 1885. Unfortunately, colonization by the Belgians had in no way prepared the country for its independence on the 30th June 1960, as no real infrastructure had been established. The first post-independence Government, headed by Joseph Kasavubu and Patrice Lamumba, lasted less than six months, collapsing under the pressure of tribal and factional disputes. The military leader Colonel Joseph Desire Mobutu (who later changed his name to Mobutu Sese Seko) then established a civilian Government. However, when Lamumba was subsequently murdered, his followers, calling themselves Simbas (from the Swahili word for lions), formed a rebel army and stirred up hatred against any non-nationals in the north-east of the country. This included Belgians who had not yet left, missionaries and traders. The antagonism escalated and finally came to a head in 1964 with the killing of many non-nationals, including missionaries and their families still in the area.

For a while after Independence Day life in Nebobongo went on as usual. Elsie and Helen were reminded of Belgian Congo's new independence in an unusual way. As they were talking, two young children approached them with a bunch of flowers and said, 'Welcome to our country!' Then one day, as they were working in the operating theatre, a distressed missionary arrived to give the alarming news that there were violent disturbances at the nearest official Government outpost. John and Elsie and all the team were called to go to Ibambi, where there was an emergency meeting with the acting Field Leader. There was much prayer and it was decided that those who were due for furlough, including John and Elsie and family, should leave immediately, together with the younger single women. One reason for this decision was the need to reduce the number of missionaries in the area so that, should trouble erupt, local Christians would not have responsibility for the safety of so many expatriates. Having so recently returned from furlough, Helen stayed on in Nebobongo.

Leaving in such haste caused much emotional trauma for John and Elsie. They were both so involved in training programmes, and caring for those in need. Travelling in convoy with other colleagues in their cars, and with no visible protection, they were very conscious of many people praying and trusting in God's care. Prayers were answered. Not long before they left, someone in the USA had sent a parcel of small tins of prepared baby food. This was needed to feed baby Lois on the long journey. At one stage on the journey they came to a Simba army camp, where others travelling through had been harassed. God sent a heavy downpour as they passed through, and no one came out to trouble them. They were able to cross the border into Uganda, where they were cared for by the Red Cross.

Following the long journey, which had involved many long hours of driving with very little sleep, John became ill. It so happened that a doctor, with whom he had trained, was working locally and came to see if there was any way he could help the refugees. After seeing John in a state of exhaustion, he felt that rest was needed. The doctor took him to his home to recover. He recommended that a sea voyage would be beneficial to John, and this was arranged. Meanwhile, Elsie boarded a plane for England, with David aged three and a half and Lois aged nine months. Elsie had not flown before, and going home leaving John in Africa was not something she had envisaged or wanted. It was one of many further separations. But the six-week voyage was just what was needed to get John up and running again.

5

'Now I Can Sell My Fish'

Home leave can be full of strain and stress, in spite of the joy of seeing family and friends and being in a land of comparative plenty. For David and Lois, this was their first experience of life outside Africa. David, at three and a half, was delighted with all his new discoveries, but there were adjustments to make in the way things were done. His Aunt Grace once took him out shopping and had asked him to remind her to buy oranges. While in the market, as Grace was talking to a friend, David spotted some oranges and started to fill her basket from the stall. The stallholder was not impressed!

John was well now, but Elsie had to spend two weeks being treated for filaria. It was on one of John's visits to her in hospital that he broke the news about their next assignment. The war in Belgian Congo had made it impossible for them to return there. The north-east of the country, where they had worked, was badly affected by the violence. But John had been offered further training in the treatment of leprosy in India, and was overjoyed.

★ ★ ★ ★ ★

In 1961, after eleven months in England, the family set sail for another continent to adjust to a new language, a different culture and another group of colleagues. The last part of

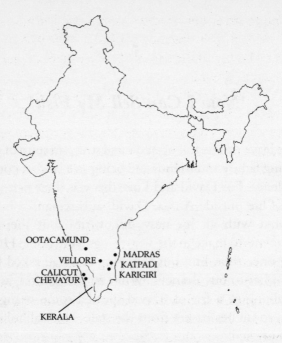

India

their journey was by train from Madras to Katpadi, not far from where the training centre was situated. Their arrival was eagerly anticipated as Ruth, John's eldest sister, was to be waiting for them on the platform. Ruth and Monica, another sister, had already been in India for some years. Elsie remembers the reunion well, as it nearly ended in disaster. John was leaning out of the window searching for his sister on the crowded platform. He called out to Elsie, 'There she is!', but as Ruth ran towards them she tripped over a box and fell to the ground. She had been so intent on running to greet her brother, whom she had not seen for many years, that she had not noticed it. Fortunately she was not badly hurt, and she had her brother there to pick her up and dust her down!

As they travelled by car to the training centre in Karigiri there was so much to notice that was very different from African scenes. There were vast numbers of people everywhere, and bullock carts, sometimes carrying drivers who were fast asleep! It was a relief to reach Karigiri, but somewhere along the line there had been a lack of communication and they were not expected. They were rather embarrassed when a young, single man was asked to vacate his home temporarily and move in with someone else so that the new family could have somewhere to live. Hopefully he did not mind when he realized their plight!

John quickly settled into the routine of being an eager student. He had the capacity to give himself wholly to whatever lay before him. Elsie set up home and helped the children to adjust to India, not least to the heat. She carried out various jobs using her secretarial and nursing skills, and learned some physiotherapy, which was essential for leprosy patients undergoing surgical treatment for deformities. Soon John and Elsie were given a house suitable for their family, enabling the single man to return to his home.

After fifteen months in Karigiri, just as they were feeling settled in their home and work, they were asked to move to Vellore Christian Medical College a few kilometres away. David had been travelling to school in Vellore each day. To his delight, John was to work in the Hand Research Unit, where Paul Brand was pioneering operations for correction of hand deformities. Everything was prepared for John to slot into his new job, but again there was no family home for them to occupy! They were put up in what was known as number 5, 'A' line – accommodation designed for Indian students, who were mostly single men. They had very limited space, and the children slept on camp beds, but the friendship and help of the people around made up for the rather spartan accommodation. John learnt much from Paul, and Elsie had the challenge and joy of leading Bible study with a small group of female students. John finished his training in Vellore in 1964.

★ ★ ★ ★ ★

News from Belgian Congo continued to be very disturbing. The country was in chaos, and five of John and Elsie's former colleagues were among missionaries killed by the Simbas. There was no possibility of them returning to work in Nebobongo, or anywhere else in the north-east. While they had not moved from the conviction that leprosy work was their calling, WEC did not currently have any openings for this type of medical work. However, in the South Indian state of Kerala there was a hospital called Chevayur, where leprosy patients in all stages of the disease were cared for. The hospital was situated in the town of Calicut, quite close to the sea, therefore hot and humid, but also a place of great natural beauty with coconut, cashew nut and jackfruit trees. As well as the hospital, there was a home for those who had been disowned by their families, a school for children with leprosy and a unit for people to continue treatment as out-patients after leaving the hospital. John and Elsie heard that there was a place for them at Chevayur, amongst workers with The Leprosy Mission. As they prayed and discussed this new and challenging invitation with their colleagues in WEC, the consensus was that this was a further call from the Lord. However, the decision to go to Calicut would include not only moving to another new place of work, but leaving WEC and joining The Leprosy Mission. After so many years of fellowship with WEC workers this was not an easy decision to make, but with their strong sense of calling to leprosy work John and Elsie felt that this was a step that needed to be taken.

The Leprosy Mission (TLM) had many years of experience in this field of work and working for TLM was to open up for John and Elsie a future full of opportunity in helping to alleviate the suffering of leprosy patients. They found a good spirit of co-operation among the staff at Chevayur. Elizabeth Spiess, a nurse seconded from Germany, was an inspiring person to work with. Hilde Hones, a deaconess nurse, also from Germany, was another dedicated team member. Other staff members included two trained Indian nurses, and those who were themselves leprosy patients fulfilled various roles in the hospital.

John and Elsie had many stories of patients whose lives and appearances were transformed as God gave the medical staff at Chevayur increased wisdom and expertise. One such story was of a man who was a fish seller. When he first arrived at the hospital he had been in a very bad state of health and had faced a long period of treatment. Firstly, his leprosy was treated medically, then John worked out a plan which included reconstructive surgery to correct hand and foot deformities. There followed weeks of physiotherapy and education as to how to care for his reconstructed limbs. He was delighted with all that had been done for him, but one day, after expressing his gratitude, he said sadly, 'I still cannot sell my fish; people will reject me because of my deformed face.' His face had badly been affected: he had excessive layers of skin and elongated ears. So he underwent surgery to change his appearance, not for vanity's sake, but for that of his livelihood. It was a thrilling day when he was able to look into the mirror and say with a happy smile, '*Now* I can sell my fish.'

Dr Alexander Thomas, now a consultant physician at Dayapuram Hospital in India's Tamil Nadu state, has given some insights into aspects of John's character and work during his years in India. As a medical student at Vellore Christian Medical College, he remembered John not only as an expert in reconstructive surgery.

> As a student, and later as a leprologist, I looked to him as my teacher and as a master craftsman of his trade. More than his interest in deformed hands and insensitive feet, he was deeply interested in the spiritual life of all his students, colleagues and patients. I enjoyed attending his devotional addresses in the men's hostel. He had a wide knowledge of Bible verses and he enjoyed sharing these treasures with us. I especially remember his talks on the book of Proverbs.

Dr Thomas also recalled an incident when John gently chided him for misplaced enthusiasm.

> Once, while going for an evening cycle ride, I met a leprosy patient who was walking with a big bandage on his

feet. He wanted to be admitted to the hospital but I did not know how I could be of help to this man. The only person I knew in those days was Dr Harris, so I took him on my cycle to the doctor's home. Dr Harris appreciated my enthusiasm as a student to help a patient, but quietly advised me that I should not take a patient to his home. He knew the only help that could be given to such men was not an instant solution by a doctor but the discipline of training in self-care and regular attendance at clinics.

After his graduation from Vellore, Dr Thomas was sent to Chevayur. He wrote of John's responsibilities and lifestyle at the hospital.

John . . . was responsible for the entire surgical work as well as in planning for residential quarters for the medical officers. Looking back on his three-year stay there many older patients remember his compassionate and kind services. Dr Harris was noted for his simple living and humble lifestyle. Every morning he would go for a walk to where fishermen were bringing loads of fish, carried on their heads, for sale. Sardines were cheap and Dr Harris was never ashamed to carry this fish from the market to his home, although in the local culture it was below the status of a doctor to buy sardines from the local market.

Another incident recalled by Dr Thomas demonstrates how John would have nothing to do with any transaction that involved the suspicion of a bribe. In some of the places where he worked, expectations for such 'gifts' were rather too commonplace.

Dr Harris once got into trouble with a railway ticket examiner as it seemed this official was expecting some financial gain from the foreigner. Finally this situation was settled with the help of an Indian doctor.

The above confrontation shows John's determination to abide by what he felt was biblical, whatever the practices of other Christians might be. This stance was also demonstrated in an incident recounted by Dr Gottfried Riedel.

It must have been in the mid-seventies, when our old friends John and Elsie came to see us in Germany with David and Lois. On Sunday morning we went to church, and in the afternoon we played volleyball with the children in the garden. The Harrises and our children enjoyed the game very much, with smashing and shouting and running about enthusiastically. I myself took part, forgetting my fifty-plus years. But John stood there at the edge of the field, looking alarmed and refusing to join in the game. When I asked him, 'Is there anything wrong with you?' he said gravely, 'Don't you realize it is Sunday today? On Sundays we are not supposed to play games.' As it was already tea time, we stopped playing and went back into the house. We agreed that as we, the Riedels, were free to enjoy God's gifts on Sunday, so were the Harrises free to obey the commandment literally on this day. Afterwards I thought it admirable how he stuck to an often unpopular obedience instead of yielding to the *Zeitgeist*.

By now, David and Lois had reached school age. They had learned much from their experiences of Africa, England and

India. But if John and Elsie were to stay at Chevayur, boarding school would be the next step in their education, as it was for the children of many missionary families. John and Elsie had many factors to consider in sending the children away, not least the prospect of seeing them only two or three times a year. Boarding school had many advantages for David and Lois: the company of children from their own culture, who spoke their own language, and the receiving of a good education in a Christian environment being just a few. All these advantages had to be weighed against the natural pull on the heartstrings of parents who would love to have seen their children grow up close to them, and desperately wanted to do their best for them. Yet John and Elsie felt the strong call of the Lord to stay where they were. They had a choice to make that could only be made before the Lord and carried through in His strength. At length it was decided that David, aged seven, would go to Lushington, a Christian school in Ootacamund, situated in a mountainous region two hundred miles from Calicut. Later, at the age of five and a half, Lois, who was raring to go, went to the sister school of Hebron. For the children it was an unknown and in many ways an exciting situation, although it meant the loneliness of long separations and the inability to share the daily ups and downs of life with close family. Still, there were the vacation times and the visits of John and Elsie to the school on special occasions to look forward to.

6

The Case of the Missing Idols

The next move for John and Elsie came completely out of the blue. Until 1968, they were both happily involved at Chevayur and the Lord was blessing their work among leprosy sufferers. Then came a thunderbolt! A telegram arrived from TLM asking if they would go and take over a work in Nepal. An expatriate doctor had left Anandaban Hospital suddenly, due to illness. The telegram had taken ten days to arrive, and TLM had asked for a reply on the tenth day. It was a big decision to make, with very little time to weigh up the matter.

It was clear that although John and Elsie were taken completely by surprise by this request, God was not! He had already prepared the way. An Indian doctor had recently arrived to help at Chevayur, and he would be able to carry on the work that would be left by John. John and Elsie were now familiar with change, although for Elsie it was always a struggle to find acceptance in contemplating another move. Again it would mean learning a new language, living in a different climate with people of a different culture, and setting up home in a strange environment. It would also mean that they would be around two thousand miles from the schools where David and Lois were studying. They were settled and did not want to move.

John spoke about their decision to go to Nepal in the Stewart Lecture he gave to the Christian Medical and Dental Society in Port Dickson, Malaysia, in January 1995, shortly before his death.

> We felt we should accept this as from the Lord and we were enabled to roll the whole matter on to Him to work it out, and He did. We had been prepared for this key move to an unevangelized land in several ways. We had had deep prayer interest in Nepal for several years. The situation in the hospital where we were working in India was changing ... The Lord showed me there were no more questions to be asked about whether we should go or not ... Nepal turned out to be a very wonderful five years in our lives.

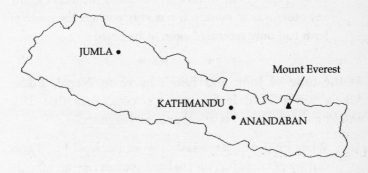

Nepal

The Hindu Kingdom of Nepal, a land closed to foreigners until 1951, abounds in temples and idols. Every town and village has its shrines to various gods. Visitors can see people bathing in a sacred river in front of the famous Temple of Pasupati Nath, in the capital city of Kathmandu, in the false hope that this will wash away their sins. Offerings are prepared for the worship of the gods.

It was a joy for John and Elsie to arrive in a country of such great need and to be involved in the relatively new area of leprosy work. Nora Vickers, who had first known John and Elsie at Mildmay Mission Hospital, met them again when she herself was a missionary in Nepal. She wrote about John's time here.

> The small leprosy hospital named Anandaban, meaning Forest of Joy, was about twelve miles from Kathmandu over a near impassable track which made it seem much further. Here John worked indefatigably (he didn't know any other way to work!). It was a place where the name of Jesus had only recently begun to be heard.

★   ★   ★   ★   ★

At the time of John and Elsie's move to Nepal, Eddie Askew was a TLM leader. He was concerned that they would have to learn yet another new language.

> When he [John] was asked to work in Nepal I told him that we didn't expect him to learn another language (he already had several under his belt). But he quickly became fluent in Nepali and I began to realize that he was counter-suggestible, and anyway, how could he share his faith

without the local language? That was always the primary motivation.

★ ★ ★ ★ ★

Howard Barclay, the Executive Director of the United Mission to Nepal, remembered how John tackled the Nepali language.

> He had no sooner arrived when he spoke of learning the language. How many he had learned before and how often is amazing! At that time he told me how he learned them best – by Scripture memorization! Once he had mastered the Devanagari script he was away! I was one of the examiners when he took his first exam. I recall that almost every answer he gave, or comment he made, was somehow associated with a verse of Scripture. When, during the exam, he had to give a short talk, it sounded like a string of Bible verses somehow brought together to apply to the theme he was given. It was marvellous, and earned him a good pass.

John and Elsie soon learned that the Nepali Government had imposed restrictions on any form of overt Christian outreach. The staff met for worship on the flat roof of the hospital, surrounded by breathtakingly beautiful views – they were on the edge of the Himalayan mountains. They were prohibited from inviting patients to join them, but if the patients wanted to come of their own accord, that was allowed. Many did come, and the staff saw the Gospel changing their lives. They soon realized that those who had been touched by the Lord were gossiping the good news to others.

Sometimes people would arrive at the hospital after walking for many days to get help. When John found that leprosy sufferers were coming from a place called Jumla, thirty days' walk away, he was granted Government permission to fly there once a month to hold a clinic.

One woman's life was completely changed at Anandaban. Marium had been carried in a conical basket on the back of a coolie (a porter, low down in the Hindu caste system) all the way from Kathmandu. As they neared the hospital the coolie had taken fright, perhaps at the thought of entering a hospital for leprosy patients, and had left her stranded on the hillside below the hospital. She had one useless leg, so was unable to climb up to the hospital. She might have died from exposure had not a hospital worker happened to pass that way and seen what looked like a blanket lying on the path. As he neared it, the blanket moved. He picked Marium up and carried her to the hospital. For years, Marium had lived alone in a hut, cut off from everyone because of her leprosy. Now she found herself being lovingly cared for, and people even touched her. She could read, and was given a copy of Mark's Gospel. As she read, God opened her eyes to the truth and she believed. She soon began to teach others. Her useless leg was amputated and she was fitted with an artificial leg, which enabled her to be mobile. Even though she had hand deformities she could hold a pen and eventually she was able to help Wycliffe Bible Translators with their translation of the New Testament into the Newari language. John and Elsie met Marium again when they attended a TLM conference in Nepal nearly twenty years later. What a joyful reunion that was! They found she was happily married and she and her husband had adopted a small boy.

In 1970, the Christians at Anandaban experienced a time of acute testing. A number of disasters struck the work in the space of a few days. It all started when a local man asked to be baptized. Almost immediately a false accusation was filed against John: that he had incited the villagers to steal twenty-four antique Hindu idols, probably worth approximately £24,000 then. At about the same time a landslide cut off the water supply to the hospital, the generator stopped functioning and the hospital's Land Rover developed problems that made it unusable.

Quite how a man asking for baptism triggered John's being accused of theft was never fully understood. The plot was hatched by a local man who lived in the valley below the hospital (from where the man who had asked for baptism also came). It was thought that the perpetrator made his plans after hearing of the intended baptism, with the intention of destroying the hospital. The stigma attached to leprosy was great – many believed it to be a curse from the gods. Having stolen the idols, the man stirred up the local people to believe his accusation that the doctor was guilty of theft. This gave him time to attempt to sell the idols and make a large amount of money.

Officials came to search the hospital and staff houses. John was taken into police custody and kept there for ten days, leaving the hospital without a doctor. Three of the staff were also accused, and were beaten and questioned but faithfully defended their doctor, denying he had had any part in this deed. John was twice taken to the village from where the idols had been stolen, where he was reviled and spat on. He felt he was only saved from lynching by the Lord's protection. There was talk about destroying the hospital. Elsie was understandably anxious as the rumour went round that they might be deported from the country. She received tremendous support from young Nepali believers among the patients, who never doubted that God would protect their doctor and bring him back.

Howard Barclay proved to be a real friend during this time of great stress. When he heard about the crisis he came to Anandaban immediately. He helped in many practical ways, and gave loving support to Elsie and the staff. He has vivid memories of this time.

> I went to the court hearings. It was a time of deep suffering for Christ. The case went on for some time. On one occasion I recall talking to the magistrate, and in order to make a point I asked him, a very high caste Brahmin, if he ever ate beef. This was unthinkable to him. I pointed out that for John, the accusation that he had anything to do with idols was worse than an accusation of the magistrates eating beef! He didn't answer but looked thoughtful. At the last hearing the three men from the hospital were again interrogated. The youngest was a boy of fifteen and he spoke up strongly and totally denied any involvement in the theft by himself or by Dr Harris. It was completely unexpected, and very brave of the young lad. No doubt this was an answer to many prayers. The case collapsed and John and the others were publicly exonerated and freed. Immediately John beamed and gave glory to God.

In answer to the prayers of Christians in countries all over the world, God had intervened. The idols were found in a building at the airport awaiting transport abroad. John and the three other accused staff members returned to the hospital to join in the celebration of God's act of deliverance. The rocks blocking the road were blasted away, the water system was repaired, the generator was fixed and the Land Rover was again able to take to the road. The work in Nepal continued with God's blessing.

Many years later, when giving the Stewart Lecture, John looked back on this testing time.

> God will vindicate the sincere obedience of His children. God, who is love, is in control in a special way in medical missions, carried out in Jesus' name. Let us recognize the evidence when He faithfully vindicates us. And the basis of it all is surely Calvary and God's vindication of His own Son by raising Him from the dead. Although medical work, done in the name of Jesus, will be bitterly opposed, especially in countries without a Christian witness, God is able to reverse totally the gloomiest situations bringing enormous encouragement.

James Nakami was a Nepali Christian who was chosen by John to work in the hospital. Despite his hearing problem, James's appointment reaped many rewards for the hospital as he proved to be a very gifted man, and an excellent teacher. His appointment also encouraged other local people to seek employment at the hospital, as he proved to them that leprosy was not contagious. James's memories of John are still vivid.

Dr John Harris was not only a surgeon but also a deeply spiritual person. He was a devoted lover of patients and scattered spiritual seeds in Nepal. He sat with the leprosy patients whom many thought were highly infectious. He was a human being like me and I was helped by his lovely natural character. I learned from him how to make leprosy patients happy.

James also recalled the clinic John started in the remote area of Jumla.

At these clinics more than two hundred patients were registered for treatment. They were amazed to find that leprosy was a curable disease. They got new lives and later often asked me when Dr Harris would come back to Nepal.

Eileen Lodge, a veteran missionary, served the Lord in Nepal for many years. She recalled working with John.

John will always be remembered with great affection by the patients that were with him in Anandaban. He was a friend to all, and they knew that he empathized with them in their suffering. But more than that, he showed them the way to the love of God, which was healing to them in every way. I, for one, remember John with real affection.

The years that John and Elsie spent in Nepal meant a long separation from their children. But for David and Lois, there were compensations. During the long twice-yearly holidays they had the freedom to roam and play on the hillsides for hours on end. There was no need to learn rules about crossing the road, or being wary of strangers – these people were their friends.

John wanted his children to be courageous. One day, David was playing with a friend, Trevor, who had no fear and sometimes did things that could have ended in disaster. Trevor's parents were missionary friends of John and Elsie. They had seven boys, all daredevils. On one occasion, Trevor decided to accept the challenge of walking across a pipe spanning a forty-five foot drop above a stream. David followed, but shuffled across on his hands and knees. When this exploit was recounted at home, John said, 'Didn't you walk across?' David had expected a rebuke for being fool-hardy!

Aged fourteen, David and two other boys from his school went on a trek in the Himalayan mountains with a teacher, Brian Wood. David remembers his disappointment when his father's commitment to his work in the hospital prevented him from joining the expedition. John must have agonized over this decision, as David begged him to go. To John, the priority, in this instance, lay with the hospital and his patients. To David, though, it seemed that his father wrongly thought that the running of the hospital depended on him. The trek proved exciting, and dangerous at times. Brian Wood was a man of tremendous character and he influenced his fellow trekkers for good. Sadly, he died on a later mountaineering expedition.

7

An Unforgettable Journey

By 1973, John and Elsie had completed five full and fruitful years in Nepal. Now they were due for furlough again. On arrival in the UK there was much to plan, and again there were decisions to be made in relation to the future of the family. David was to go to school in the UK to study for his A levels, as was Lois, who was embarking on her O levels.

When John and Elsie were called for debriefing sessions at TLM they were surprised to hear people commenting that perhaps they had been overzealous in their ministry. It was suggested that the idols case might have been brought on by their own unwise actions. For John and Elsie this proved to be a very testing time, as it seemed that there was general misunderstanding of the details surrounding the incident. John took all this calmly and never attempted to defend his position. Elsie found it all very upsetting. They were both comforted in the assurance that they had acted wisely, had never entered a Hindu temple, or broken any Nepali law. They had carried out the leprosy work entrusted to them with joy. They trusted the Lord to turn this potential source of bitterness into blessing, but acceptance did not come easily. At this time they were living in a flat (belonging to TLM) in Kew, and it was during many hours spent walking in Kew Gardens that the Lord drew near to them to refresh them in body, mind and spirit.

When they left Anandaban John and Elsie had expected to return there after home leave. John was a good communicator of the Nepali language and there were still many challenges waiting for them in Nepal. Perhaps partly because of the spiritual battles they had been through with their Nepali brothers and sisters, they had put down deep roots there. But as the time came to prepare to return, they once again found themselves faced with redirection. TLM had recently surveyed Zaire (as Belgian Congo had been named since 1971) and had found that leprosy work was in chaos in the aftermath of the Simba war. There were now openings for missionaries to return, and John and Elsie were asked to consider revisiting the area to assess the country's needs and help organize the programme of leprosy work. It was fourteen years since they had left, but they had the qualifications and the languages needed. Returning to a land where some of their dear colleagues had been killed was not a prospect that excited Elsie, but once again they sought the Lord's will, and knew that they had been commissioned.

However, as David and Lois were now studying in the UK, John and Elsie came to the conclusion that it would be best for the family if Elsie were to stay on at the flat in Kew, to make a temporary home for them.

In 1974, John set off for Zaire alone. He was aware that he faced a formidable task. He did not know how he was going to tackle what lay ahead, nor did he know that it was in God's plan that during the next twenty-one years all his training and experience would brought into fruition. The outcome would be the establishment of a leprosy programme resulting in a dramatic fall in the prevalence of leprosy in north-east Zaire. Eventually there would be only a few patients requiring reconstructive surgery left.

Eddie Askew revealed how John's decision to return to Zaire came about, from TLM's point of view.

> During this time, after the Simba rebellion, leprosy work in much of Zaire was badly disrupted and conditions and treatment for patients very poor. I saw this for myself on a couple of extended visits. I felt that John was the man to get things going again, but I knew better than to ask him directly. Instead I invited him to revisit the area, assess the needs and write a report for the Mission. He did. Later we talked and prayed over the report. 'John,' I said, 'We need someone to head up this work. Do you know anyone who could do it? Please pray about it.' A few days later he came back to the office. 'I'll go,' he said. Like this one, all his decisions had to be dictated by God, not necessarily directed by the Mission! And the reorganization of the leprosy work in that area began, expanded, continued and was blessed through the work that he and Elsie continued until his death.

On arrival in Zaire, and after talking with others, John began to work out a plan to re-establish a system for the treatment of leprosy in such a large area of the country. There were many questions to be answered. What were the priorities? Where should the programme be based? To which part of the programme should John devote his time? As people prayed, each one of these questions was answered. John began by laying plans to train Christian men who could go and live in remote places, seek out early cases of leprosy and treat patients before deformities occurred. With the new drugs available, patients diagnosed early could be completely cured. The workers could also be trained to treat patients who already had deformities, and to instruct them on how to care for themselves.

The need for suitable men was made known to church leaders and health committees in the area. Students were chosen for the first three-month course in the diagnosis and treatment of leprosy. John selected those who loved the Lord Jesus and wanted to help leprosy patients. The place chosen in which to hold the course was an old building at Nyankunde Medical Centre. Elsie had visited Nyankunde on her journey to Ibambi in 1955. The teaching started unobtrusively, with no launching ceremony. The plan was to have one such course each year. At the end of the three months, after the students went to their assigned places of work, John visited each newly trained paramedic to give them on-the-spot help and to disciple them in their walk with the Lord. John had no permanent place to live as he was on the move so much. After nine months in Zaire, he would spend three months in the UK with his family. This was the pattern for the next three and a half years.

In 1978, John and Elsie decided to return to Nyankunde together. David and Lois were also at stages in their careers where they could take a break. They had both been born in Zaire, but, being so young when the family had moved to India, they did not remember the country. Both were eager to go back to see their roots, which they could now do as a family. But the journey was not to be an overnight flight! Something far more exciting and adventurous was planned. TLM had a new Land Rover, a gift to an Africa Inland Mission (AIM) centre in Banda, north-east Zaire – a place John visited regularly to oversee the leprosy work. After much prayer and consultation with TLM and the family, John and Elsie offered to take it out. The advantages of such a journey were manifold: they could spend time together as a family, visit the places where David and Lois were born as well as new areas of Africa, and discuss leprosy treatment with workers *en route*. They weighed up the advantages against the physical stamina that would be needed. Should Elsie return to Africa by air while John, David and Lois went by land? (This was John's idea, not Elsie's!) In spite of the rigours of the journey, the decision to go by land as a complete family proved to be the right one. What would they have done without Elsie!

Once the decision to go was made the maps came out and John and David spent time planning the route they would take. The shortest and usual itinerary in such expeditions was to cross the Mediterranean Sea and travel south on a well-known route along the eastern side of the Sahara. But David, a young man eager for adventure, suggested they go a different way – through West Africa. He doubted that his father would consider such an idea, as it would mean much longer on the road. But John found the suggestion challenging and agreed, no doubt thinking of all the countries they would pass through where he would find those who needed help treating leprosy patients. It was good that the hazards and adventures that awaited them were not known to them then!

Preparations for the adventure included obtaining visas for around ten countries, writing letters to those they would visit and buying provisions for a journey which in the event lasted for over eight weeks. John found out that they would need to travel by boat as far as Dakar, in Senegal, as there was war amongst tribes on the north-west borders of the Sahara. He was able to book passages on a boat that travelled from Marseilles to Dakar, where they would begin the journey across Africa to Zaire.

Even before they set out, God's providence was at work. Modifications had to be made to the Land Rover as they were heavily laden with equipment for the work, as well as personal luggage. Larry O'Neill, a bus mechanic and a member of South Ealing Mission, had the inspired idea of putting in a bar behind the seats to help secure the luggage. Only God knew that this was destined to protect them from serious injury a few weeks later.

On the 29th September 1978 a group of relatives, people from South Ealing Mission and Leprosy Mission friends gathered outside TLM house in Kew to say farewell. The momentous journey was committed to the Lord, and they were off.

The first challenge of the journey occurred after they had passed uneventfully through customs at Dover and were safely on board and heading for Calais. John realized that he had forgotten to obtain the Land Rover excise form. The purser on the boat gloomily predicted that they would have to return to Dover with the Land Rover and start again! But

The Harris family setting off on the Land Rover journey across
Africa.

the customs official at Calais waved them through when he
was shown another paper that seemed to satisfy bureaucratic
requirements. His comment was, 'Ici, pas de problème,'
and, as they set out, their response was, 'Thank you, Lord!'
Now on dry land, they set out on a long journey to
Courrieres in France, where they were warmly welcomed
by Robert and Ivy Milliken. Reminiscences came thick and
fast! Their last meeting had been in Malingwia, where the
Millikens had welcomed John when he had arrived as a
new, single missionary twenty-five years earlier. Robert
was now pastoring a small church whose members had been
praying for the family and their leprosy work. They were

delighted to see slides and to hear first-hand of the needs for prayer. The church gave a gift for the work, and the next morning sent the travellers off on the next stage of the journey, to Marseilles, where they boarded a boat for the six-day journey to Dakar. They travelled in economy-class, behind the funnels, which constantly covered them with black smuts. Most expatriates travelled first-class, but there was one other family travelling with the Harrises. They were going to Senegal for the first time. Their adaptation to Africa started right there on the boat – the economy-class chef catered only for African tastes. After a day or two of what seemed a rather monotonous diet, Elsie had an idea. They had brought with them a cake to celebrate David and Lois's birthdays, which were in October. Why not celebrate early with the other family? It was a delicious culinary treat, and helped to see them all through the next few days of local food.

The heat and humidity in Dakar was stifling. The Harrises gratefully accepted hospitality from a WEC missionary, who helped John through the seven-hour ordeal of paperwork in order to get the Land Rover off the boat. The family was longing to get moving, but there was a major problem. The road from Dakar to Bamako, in Mali, was impassable because of heavy rain, and the trains were all full. The only way to continue the journey was to hire a truck on a goods train. There were two other car owners in the same predicament: one was a Belgian civil servant, the other a Roman Catholic priest who was travelling with a nun. A truck was found and a price agreed. But there was a further payment required, which John saw as amounting to a bribe.

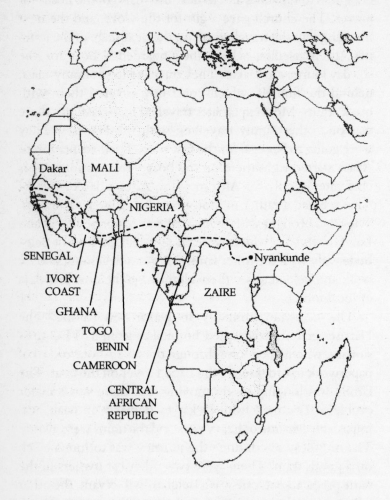

Route taken by the Harris family on their journey across Africa.

He was not prepared to contribute to this as a matter of con-science. David remembers this causing a frosty atmosphere amongst the other travellers, but they finally settled the matter and the vehicles were loaded on board the truck and secured by wire. It was boiling hot and the WEC missionar-ies waving them off took pity on them, donating two straw hats and four straw fans to relieve their discomfort. The journey of two days and nights was far from five-star! John and Elsie slept in the Land Rover with all the luggage, and David and Lois slept on top. As the train jolted and swayed, Elsie feared that they might roll off in the night. David calmed her fears by assuring her that he had fastened himself to the rail on the side of the Land Rover, and had fastened Lois to him. Their food was running out, but there were cheap bananas for sale at stops along the way and in spite of Lois's protestations, they became the family's main source of nutrition. John saw it as a priority to keep his family eating fruit, whatever else might be lacking in their diet!

At last they were able to hit the road, and drove on through the French speaking-countries of Mali and Ivory Coast, then through Ghana, Toga, Benin, Nigeria and Cameroon. They spent about ten hours travelling each day. Hospitality at the mission centres, guesthouses and other places where they stopped was outstandingly generous. One evening, shortly after their arrival in Nigeria, the family stopped off at the home of a Christian man who was working as a United Nations representative in Lagos. His duties meant he was out when they arrived, but his Nige-rian househelper gave them a lovely African welcome and produced a hearty meal to revive them. Their host soon arrived home and they had a wonderful time of fellowship. He had a long-standing interest in TLM, and he and John talked well into the night. They were also told about the novel way in which the enormous traffic problem in Lagos was being dealt with. Cars with odd number plates could travel on one day, and those with even number plates on the next. Having arrived on the right day for their car, they might have had to wait an extra day. But their host, being a UN worker, was able to give them a permit to allow them to travel.

On one occasion the family's arrival caused some consternation. A young English missionary couple living in a remote place had received a letter some weeks before, giving the probable date of their visit. In the midst of a busy life they had put it in the waste-paper basket, not really believing that such a journey would prove possible. When the Land Rover drove up late one afternoon, they were amazed. They felt totally unprepared, especially as their guesthouse had not been used for a long time – visitors rarely came their way. Once convinced that they were not dreaming, they opened up the guesthouse and made preparations for the family to stay the night. There was no time to remove the cobwebs hanging from the ceiling, or to evict all the creepy-crawlies that had lived there, undisturbed, for so long, but the family was grateful for the welcome they received and the effort made to provide hospitality. Their hosts could hardly pop round to the local supermarket or Chinese takeaway for ready meals, but they provided a satisfying meal for them all from what they had, even if it took time to get it together. David remembers John commending their generous sharing of provisions, which perhaps had left them with not too much until their next shopping expedition. In the morning, the couple took them round the nearby old Muslim town and other places of interest, and then saw them take to the road again, no doubt still suffering from shock at the seeming impossibility of such a journey.

It was while driving at night on a dry and dusty road in Cameroon that the heavily loaded vehicle skidded on a bend and ended up in the forest. It was stopped from rolling over by an ant hill – these are sizeable features of the African landscape. The luggage was prevented from sliding on top of the family by the iron bar that had been so thoughtfully fitted by the mechanic from South Ealing Mission. As they climbed out of the vehicle, unhurt, they surveyed the damage done – a smashed windscreen and side-mirror and other dents and scratches on the bodywork, but the engine was still intact. But for God's protecting hand it could have been so much worse. John's glasses had flown off into the forest and were never found, so he had to manage by the skilful use of two other pairs which, to be effective, had to be worn together. They arrived late that night at the nearest medical mission, where the doctor in charge was immersed in chairing a committee meeting. Coming to the door, no doubt curious as to who would be there at such a late hour, he found a rather dazed-looking family asking for some- where to spend the night. He gave them the key to the guesthouse. David slept on the veranda to be on the alert for thieves, as the contents of the Land Rover were only pro- tected by a tarpaulin. Elsie remembers the delayed shock effects she felt, lying in the pitch black and waking from time to time, wondering who she was, and where she had landed! The next morning the doctor, who had been pre-occupied with getting to the end of his committee meeting the night before, had time to hear the story of their miraculous deliverance from serious harm. He provided them with plastic sheeting for the windscreen and a new side-mirror was bought. The vehicle was checked for the onward journey through Cameroon and into the Central African Republic.

At several stops along the way John was able to consult with leprosy workers. He found that in some places there were no resources for training or for control work. There was a crying need for roadside clinics for leprosy and tuberculosis patients. These matters were discussed and John made careful notes of each place's prayer needs. Later, when he was appointed director of TLM's work in Africa, these brief visits contributed to his understanding of the needs and problems in western Africa.

As they travelled on through the Central African Republic the family began to experience the horrors of bad roads. They faced some nightmare situations throughout their journey, until their arrival at Nyankunde. In some places there were dozens of lorries waiting to be towed through craters the width of the road. One day, after an overnight stay in a guesthouse run by two Swedish ladies, they had to be towed out of holes several times and the next day were stuck for three hours as five cars were waiting to be towed. Eventually they managed to find a way round to continue on the journey. There was always the fear that they would get stuck for good! Waiting one day in a queue, a young tourist was heard to remark, 'Whatever is that older woman doing in the back of that Land Rover?' Perhaps Elsie sometimes wondered herself!

One of the biggest challenges of the journey came when they reached the border of the Central African Republic with Zaire. There was a wide and fast-flowing river to cross, and the ferry service was no longer operating. Men came forward eagerly to assure them there was a solution – the Land Rover could be taken over on five canoes, roped together, with boards on top. There was no alternative! The first stage of this hazardous operation was to completely unload the Land Rover. All the equipment and personal possessions were put in two other dugout canoes, and Elsie and Lois were paddled over the river, wedged among the luggage. They could not help experiencing feelings of trepidation as they noticed hippos grunting around them. If one of these huge creatures should happen to come up for air under a canoe, the passengers would almost certainly join them in the water.

Meanwhile, David was given the privilege of driving the Land Rover on to the canoes, as John sat beside him praying. The men skilfully paddled across the river. The currents were strong, and they had to gauge exactly how far up-river to go in order to reach the landing stage on the other side. If they did not paddle far enough upstream, and were swept too far down-river, it would be almost impossible to bring the canoes and their heavy load back again. John and David watched, fascinated by their great skill. The precarious operation of lifting the Land Rover off the canoes was completed successfully by thirty men. Having laboriously repacked everything again under the boiling sun, they were off, with thankful hearts for a safe crossing.

But there was another test of endurance ahead. As they drove up the hill from the river and rounded the next bend, they found Zairean customs awaiting them. They were told to unpack everything again for a thorough and exhaustive search of all they had brought with them. This was the most rigorous customs check they had encountered so far. They could not resist this operation, but it was frustrating to think that the customs officials must have known of the river crossing and the exertion needed to load and reload. They did not feel any warmth in the welcome offered and were glad to be on their way again, at last in the country of their destination.

The days that followed could only be described as unending experiences of rain and spending hours stuck on roads waiting in long queues to get through enormous holes in the road. On one occasion they had to wait from 10 p.m. until 4 a.m., huddled up by the road with mosquitoes making the most of such sitting targets. But God had prepared many encouragements for them along the way. There was generous hospitality, and no shortage of mechanics willing to check the Land Rover. Their arrival for the next ferry crossing was wonderfully timed. A lorry driver had been waiting for three days to cross, but they arrived on the day the ferry went. Then, one evening at around 8 p.m., they arrived in Malingwia. The welcome they received was overwhelming. After darkness has fallen in Africa, people usually stay at home, but the news of the family's arrival spread around the village in a truly African fashion. In next to no time people were gathering around them, crying, 'Our son has come home!' This was indeed a homecoming – John and Elsie had been married in Malingwia, and it was David's birthplace. As the people crowded round, David could only watch with amazement as his father demonstrated his genuine love and concern for people who were, in many cases, grossly deformed by the ravages of leprosy. He did not just politely greet them from a distance, but returned their embraces, even those who had no hands that could be shaken or whose faces were deeply scared and lacking in features. This was a genuine relationship of love and trust, shown through physical contact. For David, a young man for whom the word 'leprosy' had associations of contagion and isolation, it was a sight he would never forget.

It was soon Lois's turn to see her birthplace. On their arrival in Nebobongo a few days later, they found an equally warm and loving welcome. There was much celebrating and praising the Lord in song, and one song had been composed especially for Lois – a child of the village. At this point, John had to leave the family and fly off on an assignment for TLM. Feeling bereft without him, Elsie, David and Lois stayed on for a week until news came through on the radio that the road between Nebobongo and Nyankunde was drying out after the heavy rain. As they set off they were advised to be cautious, but it turned out that patience was needed even more than caution. As David took on the driving, more adventures awaited them.

One evening, as they neared their destination for the night, they rounded a corner to find that two large tree trunks had fallen across the road. There was no way round them. Elsie's first reaction was that they would have to return to Nebobongo, as going on seemed an impossibility to her – but it wasn't to God. They had a meal, using their camping stove, and then settled down to try and sleep in the Land Rover. Just before dawn, a truck full of young soldiers drove up on the other side of the tree trunks. Their chief officer was in a hurry and ordered the men to cut through the trunks. Axes were produced and the road was cleared in no time. The journey along the remote forest road continued, but their troubles were by no means over. Rain had again fallen in deluges. There were many lines of trucks and lorries waiting to be pulled through the huge holes in the road. Then another disaster struck. As they were waiting in a long queue, Elsie was stung by a large black ant and had a severe allergic reaction. She could hardly swallow, her pulse raced and she felt faint. David and Lois rallied round, doing all they could to alleviate her symptoms. David found a Greek merchant who, when he heard of Elsie's serious condition, assumed a commanding manner and ordered the other vehicles to allow the Land Rover passage to the rim of the hole. He then organized a chain and rope gang to lower the truck into the crater and pull it up the other side. The lorries waiting their turn to cross on the far side made room for them to journey on. God's mercy was also shown in Elsie's speedy recovery. It was a relief to arrive at the mission centre of Lolwa to rest, have a good meal and, luxury of luxuries, to have a bath.

After a few more negotiations through and around minor craters, the family finally came out of the forest and on to the grasslands, and arrived at Nyankunde on the evening of the 19th November 1978. Soon John arrived to be with them, and joined the prayers of thankfulness to God for His protecting hand through so many dangers. In spite of everything the journey had been worthwhile, not just for the many new experiences and new friends made along the way, but because of the opportunity to see the faithfulness of God. He had done what He had promised, above all that could be asked. The family had realized their utter vulnerability and had been upheld by the daily prayers of friends around the world. A precious personal memory for John and Elsie was seeing the inner strength given to David and Lois to enable them to cope in times of crisis.

The Land Rover was restored to almost pristine glory and driven to the mission centre in Banda where for many years it did sterling service. When hard work and bad roads had taken their toll and it was no longer fit for such service, it was bought by a pilot, who also worked as a game warden. His intention was to make use of the spare parts, but eventually he had the vehicle reconstructed and used it to take visitors around a game park. He sent a photo to John and Elsie (especially for David to see) to prove it was still in action!

David stayed at Nyankunde for three months, working on a church farming project and absorbing the atmosphere of the country of his birth. Lois stayed for longer and helped wherever she could, especially in the pharmacy. A medical student, Richard Wilson, arrived to do his elective period at

the centre. As John had noticed Elsie many years ago at
Mildmay Mission Hospital, Richard noticed Lois and a
friendship developed which led to their marriage in 1983.
Richard's parents were long-standing prayer supporters of
TLM. David married Elizabeth Stafford in 1985. She, too,
had roots in Africa as she was the daughter of Church Missionary Society missionaries and had been born in Kenya.

8

Living for God in a Diverse Community

As the family settled in at Nyankunde, Elsie could hardly believe that she was in the same place that she had visited twenty-three years earlier as a young missionary. From being the small centre run by Mr and Mrs Deans, reaching out to local tribes and operating a printing press, Nyankunde had burgeoned into an extensive medical teaching centre.

After the Simba uprising had eventually died down and mission work had been able to start again, Helen Roseveare and another doctor, Carl Becker, had used their experience and skills to initiate medical training programmes for African nationals. There were five founding missions, and by the time John and Elsie returned to Nyankunde together in 1978, personnel (including: doctors, nurses, pilots, accountants, teachers, technicians and mechanics) was coming from many different countries. The work was expanding rapidly, not only on the medical side, but also the printing work and the schools, still run by the Brethren Mission. TLM, with John and Elsie as their representatives, were there to bring practical help to all leprosy sufferers in the different areas overseen by each mission working in north-east Zaire.

TLM built a house for the Harrises, situated on the hill-top overlooking the centre – this home came to be known by some as 'Harris Heights'. There were no administrative buildings, so John and Elsie mainly worked from home, although John did acquire a small room near to the hospital, which he used for work. A visitor from the UK remembers being shown this room, and John asking what could be done to make it more attractive. A coat of paint was suggested. John looked rather astonished, and said, 'But it has just been whitewashed!' At least he did not have to agonize over sheets of colour choices, or decide if matt or gloss paint would look best!

Philip Wood, a surgeon, had arrived at Nyankunde with his wife Nancy, also a doctor, before John and Elsie set up home there. He greatly valued his friendship and partnership with John, and wrote about their time at Nyankunde.

> 'I'd like you to meet Dr John Harris.'
>
> Well, you didn't take too much notice of new visitors to Nyankunde because they were numerous and few stayed for more than a short time. John did, however, stand out, because of a warm and genuine smile and because he seemed more sincerely interested in what we were doing than many other visitors.
>
> In the summer of 1974 we had 'Mr Leprosy,' Dr Stanley Browne, visit Nyankunde to give a one-week seminar on leprosy. Some twenty-five nurses and doctors came from all over the north-east to receive in-depth, yet very practical training, that was oriented to the medical realities in Zaire. Dr Browne had worked for many years at

Yakusu, some eight hundred and fifty kilometres to the west of Nyankunde. Nyankunde had a small leprosarium for those with advanced deformities, but Stanley Browne showed us that there were people with a minimal leprosy infection that we were missing in our out-patients' department. It was great that John Harris could attend part of this leprosy seminar, since he had recently left Nepal. The medical staff gave John a very warm welcome and an invitation to join the staff permanently, with his wife, Elsie. That offer was felt to be from the Lord and was gladly accepted.

My wife, Nancy, and I were relatively new to Africa and needed much more orientation to medical work on the continent. John had joined Nyankunde after us, but he had much more experience of Zaire in the years gone by. Not long after he arrived we determined to go together to do a five-thousand-kilometre tour of the north-east by Land Rover, with the object of visiting some outlying medical stations, gaining more insights into the prevalence of leprosy, and as an educational experience for ourselves and some nursing students. We selected three male nursing students from three of the churches founded by missions that co-operated at Nyankunde. They were called Odhipio, Chwekabo and Kobinama. That was quite some trip! We were able to help literally hundreds of patients. I saw men who wanted to see a doctor for general conditions, Nancy saw any women and children, and John consulted with those with skin problems, including leprosy.

Some of the roads we travelled on have now grown back into the jungle, but even then they were in bad shape.

At one point, we slipped off the road into a marsh, miles from any village. We constructed a corduroy road from jungle-cut poles, wedged under the wheels of the Land Rover, but we could not get it out of the mess. John, as usual, was the one to suggest another time of prayer, and low and behold, a huge African suddenly appeared. I sincerely believe he was an angel from God. He immediately took charge of the situation, and got us all positioned round the Land Rover with Nancy at the controls. He let out a great bellow, which encouraged us all to push harder than before, and the Land Rover was back on the track again.

I was the Director of the nursing school at Nyankunde, and John gave lectures to our nursing students. We usually had about one-hundred of them in a four-year programme. After a while, John started his own programme for training leprosy technicians and I believe that this multiplication of effort was a major factor in greatly reducing the amount of leprosy in the area.

Amazingly, though, I do not think that John will be most remembered for his medical work in Zaire, but for his Christian testimony. These were difficult times, when the country was going downhill under President Mobutu [who had seized power in 1965]. John had a wonderful way of keeping his eyes on the Lord and of encouraging us all to do the same. He would see the spiritual side of every problem and would be a marvellous support in prayer. John would always be an encouragement and offer sound advice.

John and Elsie lived just up the hill from us. They were aunt and uncle to our children and father and mother to us. We look back on some very happy years and thank God for His presence among us in John Harris.

'I'd like you to meet Dr John Harris.'

I'm so glad I did.'

John's concern for his patients meant that he was anxious that they receive the best possible care for their physical condition. Wayne Meyers was a pathologist working in the USA, and a former missionary in Zaire. John used to send monthly biopsy samples to him. He wrote about John as a co-worker, with whom he had worked in various ways for over thirty years.

> During the last twenty years of his life, John was one of our consistent contributors in sending specimens from hundreds of well-evaluated patients. This was only one small indication of his love for those who suffer and his concern that they receive the best care possible. I always had the highest regard for John's medical acumen, but in addition, there was always in his letters and clinical descriptions an underlying expression of his interest in the things of the spirit concerning his patients. We miss opening those packages of biopsy specimens accompanied by John's personal notes and carefully documented descriptions of the patients from whom they came.

Gradually, awareness of early diagnosis and treatment of leprosy grew in the centre and beyond. There was a young woman who came to the prenatal clinic not long before her

John testing the sensitivity of a leprosy patient's feet.

baby was due. The nurse who examined her recognized that she had leprosy, resulting in her receiving treatment to arrest the disease. The painstaking teaching was also bearing fruit as, gradually, patients all over the region were diagnosed as being in the early stages of the disease, bringing them hope for a cure and a normal life.

There was no doubt that John had a God-given ability in looking after his patients. Dr Phil Fischer was John and Elsie's neighbour at Nyankunde.

> He loved his patients, and his patients loved him. He gave care that was thoughtful and competent, but was also compassionate and kind. He worked hard to make practical,

feasible interventions to help people – whether it was urging leprosy patients to get pet cats to keep the rats from chewing their toes while they slept, or whether it was advising my wife what sorts of things to drink to prevent recurring bladder infection. John's keen scientific mind was used in many ways through carefully accurate, but thoughtfully relevant, practical intervention.

John often travelled by motorbike to visit clinics. Gordon and Christine Molyneux (fellow missionaries working in the nearby town of Bunia) remember a day when one incident could well have dampened his spirits.

One of the things that characterized John was his wonderful ability to remain cheerful and positive, even in the face of adversity. Some years ago we were staying in the home of another missionary couple in Aba in the extreme north-east of what was then Zaire, and John joined us for a few days in order to do some medical work.

Every morning he would head off, rather unsteadily, on an ancient, borrowed motorbike, bumping along with a bundle of medical files strapped to the pillion. The roads were appalling – nothing more than tracks, deeply rutted and narrow and very overgrown with long couch grasses and unexpected potholes. One morning, after it had been raining heavily all night, the holes and ruts were full of mud and water. Undeterred, John set off early to cover the many miles to the nearest bush clinic. At the end of the day, and later than usual, John arrived back at the house wet and exhausted, but in good spirits. He gave us his usual cheery greeting. In answer to our enquiry about how the day had gone he exclaimed in his inimitable enthusiastic way, 'Marvellous! The Lord is good, praise the Lord.' Then he proceeded to tell us of how he had skidded and slid along the track, and all the medical files had fallen off the back of the motorbike and scattered along the roadside. Unfortunately, John did not notice the loss until he was several miles further on, so he had had to return the way he had come, searching in the long grasses to retrieve the precious files. Thankfully, he found them all and was able to continue on his way, rejoicing.

It was this unquenchable spirit and cheery disposition, coupled with his ability to see the good hand of God in every situation, which set John apart. When most of us would have been grumbling and feeling hard-done-by after such a trip, John was still praising God. What an example!

'Harris Heights' proved to be a haven of rest and refreshment, both spiritual and physical, for many. A missionary, Joy Taylor, whose husband had been killed by the Simbas in 1964, remembers the days she spent convalescing there after a bad dose of hepatitis.

As I walked into their home I felt so accepted and enveloped in love. John breezed in and out, and had a way of turning even the most mundane conversation into something uplifting. He was happy! His first love [for his Lord] never seemed to wane. It was Elsie who had a problem with him – his shirts were always disappearing when he went on his safaris into the bush! So I left 'Harris Heights' enriched, encouraged and very thankful.

Hilde Morrow wrote of her memories of when she and Edward, her husband, lived next door to 'Harris Heights'.

> He was not one for idle socializing, but when I had a need I could go to see John and Elsie. Our children had full and complete confidence in Uncle John and Aunt Elsie, and I appreciated their prayers for Kiira and Jan. John often seemed to be at hand in moments of crisis, like the time when our teenage son, Jan, was feeding bananas to our bambi. The gentle little deer must have been hungry and grabbed the banana, plus Jan's thumb. The thumb needed some medical attention. I called Judy, a capable nurse who lived next door. Her anxious behaviour and mention of rabies alarmed us. Jan lost all his colour and needed to lie down. I was not sure what to do when I saw John passing by the house. When he heard of my fear he smiled and assured us that our bambi, which he knew well, didn't have rabies. So his knowledge and calmness brought the colour back to Jan's cheeks, because he knew we could trust John's judgment.

Hilde also remembered the way that John and Elsie transformed the stony ground around their house into a delightful garden of flowers and trees.

> Our whole family will never forget the evening when we were invited to watch, for the first time, a white, delicate moonflower unfold.

However, living in a community is certainly not all sweetness and light. John and Elsie experienced many of the tensions and relationship problems that inevitably arise. Their great desire was to maintain a spirit of openness, which could only be done by spending time together with others in the context of prayer and sharing.

Sally Deans, the daughter of Mr and Mrs Deans, had returned to Nyankunde, the place of her birth, to work as a nurse. Her account of visits to 'Harris Heights' have some bearing on how this fellowship was maintained.

> I was privileged to know John and his beloved wife, Elsie, very well. While I was at Nyankunde I used to go to their house every Tuesday for an evening meal. Often we would sit outside to eat the meal and enjoy the beautiful countryside and the birds. It wouldn't be long before we were talking about the Lord and his goodness to us. After supper, Elsie would wash her hair and I would set it. When this was done we would always have a time of prayer together. That was when the real business of the evening took place. We would start out with praise to God for His goodness, then we would pour out our hearts before Him for problems of others and our own needs. It was such a precious time.
>
> John had a gentle, loving way about him that pointed our thoughts to the Master and how He would look at some problem or attitude. If I was wrong in my attitude or thinking he would tell me straight out, but in a gentle way which I have never forgotten. One incident comes to mind, in connection with two of our co-workers. When this couple went travelling, they would leave without letting anyone know, so they wouldn't have the extra bother of shopping for others – it seems a trivial thing now but it

was quite annoying then. They got a bad name among the other missionaries. On one occasion they had just come back from furlough and, contrary to most people's experience, they had been able to get their brand new car in without paying any customs. I commented on this by saying, 'Isn't it strange that these folk got their car in duty free when they are never willing to do anything for others?' John replied in a kind and gentle way, 'Sally, wasn't it wonderful of the Lord to do this for them!' My balloon of annoyance was well and truly pricked, and it was certainly for my own good.

John had a special bond with the Congolese men whom he trained to run the clinics for leprosy patients. Bakalania Songolea was one of those who, in his own words, was most privileged to be trained by John in his programme.

For a period of over ten years we worked with Dr Harris, training supervisors of the programme for the north-east region. Dr Harris had a strong influence on all of us, not because of a great knowledge, but due to his teaching skills and the special care he gave to the whole person suffering from leprosy. God's love was evident by his consideration for the patients, dispensing this care for the patients' physical, mental and spiritual needs.

We learned two practical things that contributed towards successful treatment as we worked alongside him. When a patient's case seemed unusually complicated he would quickly get to the heart of the problem and find the best solution. We noticed the way he spent time painstakingly cleaning fragments from the ulcers of patients. The second lesson was his use of every opportunity for sharing the Gospel of Jesus Christ to both the trainees and the patients. Everyone whom he trained had to learn Romans 8 as part of the course. This was in order to help us understand where we were in our spiritual lives, and to recognize the presence of God's spirit in us, ministering to the suffering people. We remember Dr Harris with much love.

John touched the lives of others among the large team running the centre. Masumbuko Kasereka had the difficult and sometimes almost impossible task of being Treasurer. He found John's prayer support to be of immense value.

As an active member of the Hospital Christian Fellowship I thank God for John, in whom I could see a very challenging practical lifestyle of a medical servant following the holy example of our Lord Jesus Christ. His reliance on prayer was unique in getting solutions to problems. Ephesians 6:18, 'Pray in the Spirit on all occasions with all kinds of prayers and requests' was a verse which I saw practically worked out in the life of John.

Handling the finances in a poor and corrupt country is not an easy job for a follower of Christ. On many occasions I felt guilty and unable to turn to God after some hot discussion with colleagues or third party delegations. Then John would suddenly appear in the office, ask for problems to pray for, and then remind me to stand firm through the Lord's mercy and righteousness. John's 'no' really meant 'no', and his 'yes' arose from his conviction after speaking in prayer to the Lord. He would often tell people, 'Let us look up!' To God alone be all the glory.

Someone once described the team relationship of John and Elsie as being like that of a string (Elsie) and a kite (John). During their early years at Nyankunde they went together to village clinics, but as time went on and more national workers were trained, John travelled more often by himself. The amount of paperwork that needed to be done had greatly increased, and Elsie stayed in the office while the 'kite' flew off. These frequent separations were not easy, but Elsie has precious memories, even of the partings. John enjoyed writing poetry, and after he had left on a journey Elsie would find a poem slipped under her pillow, usually on a pretty recycled card. The subject would relate to the part of Scripture that he was meditating on at the time. Then there was the joy of his return, as Elsie stood on the small airstrip searching the sky for the first dot to appear in the distance as the plane approached. As the door was opened, John would hop out and run straight into her arms. She remembers how on his return he always had a radiance about him, and was overflowing with things he wanted to share about his travels. Their closeness, even when separated, was fostered because they both read the same passage of Scripture daily.

On the occasion of their silver wedding anniversary, the kite flew away taking the string with it. John and Elsie set out on a long Land Rover journey to all the centres where paramedics were stationed, including WEC, AIM and Norwegian Mission stations. The highlight of their trip was their arrival in Malingwia on the day of their wedding anniversary, where, once again, they were greeted with drums and the singing of a hymn, specially written for the occasion. It was a joyful time, but very much tinged with sadness. In the evening, local Christians gathered on the veranda of the house where they were staying, and as the insects buzzed and the scents of Africa filled the air, they poured out their hearts about all the suffering of the Simba war. John and Elsie cried with them, but also rejoiced when they heard of the mercies of the Lord in carrying them through such horrors.

9

Living in the Presence of the Lord

Peter Lewis, the Pastor of Cornerstone Church in Nottingham who led the thanksgiving service for John after his death, began with the words, 'To God alone be the glory', Peter remarked that if it were possible to be angry in heaven, John would be angry if the service was not introduced with this theme. He related his efforts to persuade John to write about his life. 'Over a few years I tried quite strenuously to get John to write his memoirs. It was like pulling teeth. There was no man in the world more reluctant to talk about himself.'

John once remarked to Elsie, 'If ever I write a book, I would like to show forth the faithfulness of God in our lives.' He never did write a book, but the purpose in writing about him now must surely be that all the glory for any achievements and godliness should go to God and not to John.

John was greatly committed to prayer, but first and foremost he was committed to the Lord. Basil Norgate, a London City Missioner, felt a deep spiritual affinity with John. They met as often as possible for prayer when John was on furlough, and sometimes these meetings extended into the early hours of the morning. Basil described one such meeting as a 'day of days' for both of them.

I see from my diary that John and I made a covenant with the Lord on the 10th January 1978. John proposed it and we agreed it together. It went like this. 'I covenant to do whatever the Holy Spirit would have me to do, and to be completely at His disposal.'

This was a vow that John sought to live out in every part of his life. There could be no turning back on this promise.

Making this covenant with the Lord spurred John on in his ever-increasing desire to make His Word the foundation for his living. He had had the inestimable privilege of having been encouraged to memorize the Bible from early years. Bertie Harris's mother, who had brought up eleven children, was eager to use all means to encourage her children and grandchildren to learn verses, and even whole chapters, from the Bible by heart. She spent much time in her room in her later years, as she suffered from migraines. Visiting Grandma, with her lovely, welcoming smile, framed by the white ringlets carefully styled by her two devoted single daughters, was an uplifting experience even for the very young. However, motivation to learn a chapter of the Bible for Grandma came not from entirely pure motives of love for the Word, or even love for Grandma. For a perfect recitation, there was the reward of a bright new silver coin. So, by whatever means, John had had implanted the great truths of God's word on his mind from an early age.

Helen Roseveare was astonished by his knowledge of the Bible.

I am sure he could tell me what was in each chapter. I thought I was a fairly good student of the Word, and I loved teaching the Bible every morning to the students and others in our little Nebobongo church, but sometimes John's knowledge of Scripture could be almost intimidating.

John's vow of commitment to the Lord could only be maintained by living in His presence. During the time they worked together, Helen discovered the centrality of prayer in his life.

To me, John's outstanding contribution was his prayer life. Everything was saturated in prayer. He believed strongly and passionately that only prayer would see things done to God's glory, and prevent us from making regrettable faults and errors. I was impatient, always wanting to get on with what I saw as the next most urgent job waiting to be done. John would quietly say, 'Let's pray about it first.'

Many others who have been asked to recall their memories of John have made similar comments. Nora Vickers wrote about John's intercessory prayers.

All of us who remember John think of him first of all as a fervent intercessor. During any conversation in which matters of concern were raised he would bring out a little loose-leaf notebook from his pocket, make a note of the matter, and remark, 'we must pray about that,' and you can be sure he did! He leaves a gap in the ranks of intercessors, but he would be quick to turn us away from himself to the reminder that our great High Priest 'ever lives to intercede for us'.

Mollie Clark was Director of Personnel for TLM, and she recorded her first impressions of John.

> [He was a] man of faith who spent a lot of time in prayer. John was the only person I've ever known who every time we met prayed with me. I always felt strengthened and encouraged in the faith after our meetings.

Sally Deans wrote of the way in which John inspired her to spend time in the Lord's presence.

> He really was a man of prayer. No matter what the subject was he would always be pointing us back to the Lord with suggestions such as, 'Let's tell the Lord about it,' and, 'Let's thank the Lord right now.' He was a person who fulfilled Colossians 3:1–2 – he truly lived in the heavens … He was often misunderstood, but it never seemed to divert him. He went right on following Hebrews 12:2, fixing his eyes on Jesus.

Another colleague remembers that when he was at Nyankunde, you could always find John at prayer meetings. But John did not only involve himself in informed prayer for his own sphere of work. George Verwer of Operation Mobilisation spoke of John as one who was eager to join with people praying for witness in other parts of the world.

> Of all the missionaries I knew, John was one of those who would go out of the way to come to our prayer nights in Forest Hill [in London]. I knew he was praying for us

when he was on the field and his letters made that evident. He took a real interest in what we were doing.

But was John perhaps *too* fervent a man of prayer? There were certainly those who felt a sense of spiritual inferiority when they first encountered him, perhaps thinking, 'I believe in prayer, but this is too much! We must get on with the job in hand.' Phil Fischer, while writing about John as a man of prayer, touched on the effect that John's praying had on others.

> He was so quick to pray. When people wanted to tap into John's personal knowledge and wisdom, he turned them to the ultimate, eternal Source of knowledge and wisdom. This frustrated people sometimes, but it was beneficial, I believe, for all people at all times.

After Phil and his wife moved back to the USA, Phil returned annually to Africa to teach paediatrics.

> For me, however, my teaching visits didn't really begin until I'd walked up the hill and prayed with John. This reunion was a time to put my coming week of service into perspective, and to leave everything in God's hands. My last prayer time with John, however, was a bit different. I happened to arrive on a day between 5 and 6 p.m., when John had an appointment – an appointment with God, specifically to pray for the nation of Israel. John welcomed me and invited me to join with his heart and with God's heart as we prayed for Israel, but I saw that my concerns were only secondary and that God's heartfelt concerns came first. Even in his prayer life, John showed me lessons

for all of life. My true interest should only come in aligning myself with God's heartfelt interests.

Sometimes, John would set aside a period of time to pray for a certain country or situation. He would regard this appointment as sacred to God and no interruptions were countenanced. Once, when staying with his niece, Jane, in Zimbabwe, a phone call came through from Lois in the UK about the arrival of her and Richard's child. Jane was convinced that the Lord would understand if there was a brief interruption in John's prayer time to speak with his daughter, but she had a job convincing John this was not an ordinary interruption. Breaking into a time committed to God was a matter of serious concern to John.

Praying for their family was a priority for John and Elsie. There were, of course, brothers and sisters on both sides of the family, many of whom were in far-flung places around the world. A prayer request never went unheeded. In his times of prayer with John, Basil Norgate caught a glimpse of the depth of John's concern for his children.

> I shall never forget his intercession for the family, for David and Lois in particular. I firmly believe the experience of Genesis 26 will be theirs in the family. God Almighty blessed Isaac because of his father's prayers and obedience. I believe it will be no less for John and Elsie's children now and in the coming days.

John's prayer life was closely linked with the down-to-earth vicissitudes and traumas of daily living. People knew that he would always be willing to go to the Lord with any prayer request because he believed so fervently, and acted on the belief, that only God could change a situation. The power of prayer was certainly proved in a knife-edge situation one memorable day at Nyankunde airstrip.

MAF (Missionary Aviation Fellowship) planes frequently took off from Nyankunde airstrip, and these flights sometimes carried children, leaving to further their education. One morning, a staff member was saying goodbye to his wife and two daughters, bound for the USA. It was a sad moment of parting for the family, but the way things had to be in this isolated part of the world. The small aircraft would take them on the first leg of their journey, to Nairobi. The plane taxied down the grass runway, gathered speed and prepared to take off. Just at that moment, a dog ran on to the strip, and the undercarriage wheels hit it and were damaged – as was, no doubt, the dog. An essential part of the landing gear was rendered unusable. A plan of action was initiated on the ground as the pilot radioed his plight. He was told to fly around to lighten the load by using up the fuel. John was one of the first to arrive on the scene, and preparation was made by the medical staff for possible injury to the passengers. The maintenance staff anticipated jammed doors and possible fire. The pilot decided not to tell his passengers the nature of the emergency, just that there was a reason they had to return to the airstrip. So they sat there, blissfully unaware of the danger of their situation, but maybe wondering why they couldn't land at once. It was a long few hours for those waiting below and all were involved in fervent prayer, even as they made emergency preparations. Elsie stood with the pilot's wife as the plane circled. As last, the fuel was nearly gone. As he came in to land, God gave the pilot great skill in calculating the best way to minimize damage. The landing was gentle, and the plane rolled on to its side. No one was injured, and there was great jubilation and much praise. The mother and children set off again later in the day in another plane.

After he was appointed Africa Director for TLM in 1990, John did a great deal of travelling. He would often encounter frustrations that could disrupt the most carefully laid plans, particularly when travelling to other African countries. There was an occasion when John was due to fly to an important engagement. At the small departure airport the plane had been very much overbooked. When instructions were given to board, people surged across the tarmac and a raced up the steps to secure a seat. John joined the throng, but realized that his chances of getting a place were almost nil. As he walked across the tarmac, praying, he noticed another set of steps in place at the other end of the plane, which no one was using. Why not try them? He did, and found a seat just in time, before the plane filled up from the other end and some people were left standing. The pilot waited until those without seats had disembarked before he took off. Little did he know of the thankfulness in the heart of one of his passengers as the loaded plane sped on its way. God had heard John's cry for help and had opened his eyes to see a solution that would get him to his appointment on time.

On an earlier occasion in Nepal, John was in a small plane flying to the clinic for leprosy patients in Jumla. The pilot realized there was a storm ahead that would endanger the lives of those on board if they passed through it. He regretfully announced to his passengers that he would have to turn back. John's thoughts went to all the patients waiting at the clinic, and to the staff who had made all the arrangements. There were people who would have walked for many miles to get there on that day. He did what was, to him, the most natural thing. He asked God to change the weather! The black clouds disappeared, and the pilot flew on.

When someone knows a deep communion with God through prayer, others around are bound to be affected, like ripples spreading out from a disturbance in a pond. Phil Fischer wrote about how John's ways of working were passed on to his students. Kabagambe, a student at Nyankunde, was an example.

> Kabagambe learned about leprosy from John. But Kabagambe, in a very real sense, became a bit of John. I saw Kabagambe care for patients, read his bible, and preach the Word, but I saw John's personal style embodied in and living through Kabagambe. John's life and his relationship with God were contagious, and he transmitted himself and God through his teaching and training activities.

Attending meetings and conferences inevitably comes with the job of leadership in mission. Eddie Askew recalled John's attitude to prayer and the effect this had on a meeting in the International Office of TLM.

> For John, prayer was so real and spontaneous and as much a part of everyday life as any other conversation. It could

be disconcerting at times. There was an occasion when three of us, Newberry Fox, then General Secretary, John and I were in a TLM meeting. We were in the middle of a strong discussion on policy; I've forgotten the subject but things were getting a bit heated. Suddenly, in the middle of the discussion – actually in the middle of someone's sentence as I remember it – John simply got to his feet and began walking up and down the room, head down, eyes half closed, muttering to God. This was prayer and his way forward in the discussion. After a couple of minutes he opened his eyes, smiled and sat down. The discussion resumed on a rather sweeter note.

Sir Eric and Lady Richardson have memories of John when he was appointed Africa Director for TLM. At that time, Sir Eric was Chairman of TLM. At the earliest opportunity, John asked Sir Eric to pray for him and they went to take a walk along a canal bank where they could be quiet before God. May Richardson wrote about a time when they travelled with John to Indonesia after a conference in Singapore.

John took the opportunity to sit on the plane next to Ritva Kirra, a Finnish nurse working for TLM in Indonesia. He spent much of the flight asking her for various words in Indonesian and then the next day he did a ward round in the hospital for leprosy patients, using the words he had learnt. But our outstanding memories of John are his passion for souls, his desire for the spiritual welfare of his patients and his obvious dependence on God.

But did John enjoy the more ordinary things in life? Could he relax? No doubt his answer would have been that living in God's presence is the most invigorating place to be. However, Mollie Clark reassures us that John could find great pleasure in a day out.

> On my first visit to Africa in my new job as Personnel Director for TLM, I was met by John and Elsie in Nairobi, Kenya, and we stayed in a guesthouse there. As we had a day to wait before setting off for Uganda, John suggested we spend the time in a game park. He hired a jeep and off we went. I saw a different side of John. Free from responsibility he was childlike in his excitement and delight at the marvels of the park, and this enthusiasm really increased my own enjoyment.

Dr Dundas Moore was a member of TLM England and Wales Council, and also of the International General Council for many years. His meetings with John were at field conferences in countries around the world such as Singapore, India and Thailand. After each conference, Dundas would plan a two-week trip to a Leprosy Mission work.

> It was not unusual for the name 'Harris' to crop up; for instance the medical superintendent at Anandaban Hospital in Nepal lives in 'Harris House'. Likewise, when in southern India in a town called Calicut, we visited a Government institution for those with leprosy. Sadly, since the days when it was a TLM hospital and John and Elsie had worked there with a team of staff committed to caring, standards had deteriorated. The only shining light was a

newer block, 'Harris House', in memory of John, who had worked there many years ago. Wherever he was, be it in India, Africa or Nepal, he always left his mark, and people, patients especially, never forgot him. He had an out-and-out zeal for Christ, which was often misunderstood. He always came straight to the point when we met together and enquired of me my spiritual standing with God, and how I was walking with him. I used to write to him and each letter back reflected this interest. I also thought of him as my spiritual barometer, such was his very personal interest.

Being related to John could cause some embarrassing moments! One of his sisters met a member of South Ealing Mission, to which John and Elsie were still closely linked. The conversation went something like this.

'Isn't it wonderful about John's OBE?'

'His what?'

'Didn't you know that he is to receive this award?'

'Well, no, I didn't!'

The letter bearing the news that John was to be so recognized came with an MAF pilot to Nyankunde one day in 1993. John was away at the time, and Elsie was with him when he opened the official envelope from the Embassy in Kinshasa on his return. His first reaction was to flatly refuse such an honour. He couldn't bear the thought that attention would be drawn to him when his burning desire was to bring glory to God. However, after prayer and some practical advice from friends, he realized that in accepting this honour from the Queen he would be the representative of many others in the team who had given such dedicated and loving service to leprosy patients in Zaire. The ceremony in 1994, when the family went to Buckingham Palace, proved to be an experience that will always be treasured in the memories of Elsie, David and Lois. God gives his faithful servants many bonuses!

No one discovered what John said to the Queen during the brief moment of their encounter, but he did refer to it in his 1995 Stewart Lecture. Speaking about times when he had been in danger, or challenged, John said:

I have known the reality of God's call to me and my prayer partners and of His promise to give me the right facilities, provision, wisdom, strength, the right word or whatever was needed. This was proved in times of challenge such as a strike of workers, a tendon transfer, relations with officials, a tough medical or surgical problem, language learning, research, speaking to the Queen of England, or the nightwatchman when he let the thief in ... again and again the strength He has given renewed hope and vision. How I love Jesus!

10

'Will I See You There?'

One day in late 1994, John remarked to Elsie, 'I wonder what the Lord has in store for us in 1995? It's the first time in ten years that I have not got any candidates listed for the teaching course.' The reason for the lack of students was the difficult political situation in Zaire, which made travelling a problem. There were many uncertainties concerning the country's future as it faced deepening unrest. The terrible massacres in Rwanda had profound effects on surrounding countries.

John and Elsie, though, had no doubt that the Lord would soon reveal to them His plan for the coming year. It was not long before they found out. The request for John to give the Stewart Lecture at the conference in Malaysia was totally unexpected, and it was made possible for Elsie to go too. Looking back now, she remembers the fellowship she enjoyed and the interesting lectures she attended.

In his lecture, John spoke on Psalm 18 and the way in which God's presence was a continual encouragement to David. He told of his own experiences of such blessings throughout his work in several different cultural settings. He gave some examples of God's intervention in crisis situations, such as the time Nyankunde had been down to the end of its aspirin supply. They had prayed, and at that very time an MAF pilot had been loading his plane in Kinshasa, a thousand miles away. He had paused after loading: maybe if he a removed a few more seats he could fit in a few more boxes of medicines. What were those boxes over there? Aspirins, of course! What an encouragement to the pilot and to the medical staff when he had arrived with the precious supplies.

On the way back home from Malaysia, John and Elsie celebrated their thirty-ninth wedding anniversary in Singapore. The day was made special by a visit to the Botanical Gardens, where they saw many beautiful varieties of orchids. The next day, very early in the morning, John sprang a surprise on Elsie by saying, 'We are having breakfast in a park with the birds today.' It was a place of great beauty, and the large and colourful macaws put on a splendid performance for the visitors. On the Sunday before they left they worshipped with Singaporean friends in the basement of the Garden Hotel. A visiting singing group sang a song about nothing being too difficult for God. In future months this memory gave Elsie great spiritual comfort.

John and Elsie's next stop on their way home was Nairobi, where they met an American couple, Les and Peggy Green, who had previously worked at Nyankunde and were now visiting Africa to work among pygmy people. They were on their way to lead a seminar in the forest, and asked if John and Elsie would like to accompany them to help with the teaching and preaching. After taking time to ask if this was in God's will for them, they joyfully accepted the invitation.

Soon after arriving back at Nyankunde they flew off again to a small airstrip on the edge of the Ituri forest. Les Green had gone ahead to meet them with a tractor, in order to take them to a small mission centre in a place called Akokora. Their fellow passengers on this stretch of the journey were a group of pygmy people, and there was much hearty singing as they bumped along the track. The last part of the journey into the forest was in an even more versatile all-terrain vehicle, with no roof and very large tyres, which effortlessly carried them through small streams and over fallen tree branches to their destination – a clearing in the forest. A bamboo-leaf hut had been built for the visitors, and was large enough to accommodate the Harrises at one end and the Greens at the other. They had to bend almost double to get in, and rolling into their sleeping bags on pygmy-made bamboo beds at night, and rolling out in the morning, was a hilarious business. As there was no door to close, a fire was kept burning nearby at night to keep wild animals away. When the local chief arrived to find out what was happening, the pygmies simply extended the hut to accommodate him as well.

After they had settled into their temporary home, groups of pygmies from nine different areas of the forest arrived with their meagre belongings. Their accommodation was do-it-yourself, and John and Elsie watched the women make neat igloo-shaped dwellings for their families out of sticks and leaves. Construction of each hut took about five hours. By the time they had finished, a village had sprung up in the midst of the virgin forest and four hundred pygmies, and their children, were housed and ready for the four-day seminar. The Greens had not sought to impose a different cultural way of life on the pygmies, and on the first evening there was music and dancing around the encampment. John and Elsie felt compelled to pray earnestly as the revelry went on into the night. Then violence began among the dancers – there was chaos, and this led to general agreement that there should be no dancing the next night.

The memorable experiences of the next days were described by John and Elsie in a prayer letter to friends. They wrote of the twice-daily bible messages, the perfect weather, and their being able to observe the pygmies' lifestyle. They also ministered to the pygmies' physical needs, and checked them for signs of leprosy. On their final night, John and Elsie saw evidence of God's work amongst the pygmy people.

> We had heard that since the local chief had come for the night there would be dancing for him. When . . . folk began to gather in large numbers around our hut, John thought that perhaps it was for this. But no! There were scores of enquirers seeking the Lord, salvation, repentance and all without a pressurized appeal.

While talking to the pygmies John spoke about heaven, and asked them a number of times, 'Will I see you there?' John and Elsie returned to Nyankunde with the sure knowledge that many pygmies trusted the Lord, and that some had been born again during the seminar.

The retirement age for TLM workers was sixty-five, so John officially retired in 1990. The role of Africa Director was handed on to a successor. John held very strongly to the

conviction that there is no age for retirement from the
Lord's service, and he felt it was right to stay in Zaire and
use his remaining health, strength and experience for the
Lord's gain. He helped with various leprosy projects and
continued with the training of workers. There were many
opportunities at Nyankunde for John's skills to be used, and
not only in the area of leprosy treatment. There was a man
in the hospital whose foot was twisted, due to a birth defect.
It was in a terrible state of ulceration and it seemed inevita-
ble that it would have to be removed. After careful thought
and preparation, John decided to operate – not to remove
his foot but to correct the deformity. The foot healed, and
with the help of a physiotherapist the man was eventually
able to walk normally again.

John and Elsie had made plans to travel with TLM's
interim Africa Director to investigate cases of untreated leprosy in a place called Sankuru later in 1995. In their prayer
letter of early March telling about the forest seminar, John
and Elsie spoke about this trip, and other future plans,
encouraging their readers to 'Pray also for visits to places
where the work is flagging. We need to be sure of His time-
table for us through 1995.' But before this letter was read by
their prayer partners, John was rejoicing in the immediate
presence of the Lord.

Wednesday the 8th March 1995 began for John and Elsie
like any other day at Nyankunde. John spent the morning
in his office working on statistics – not his favourite task, but
it had to be done. Elsie heard him singing 'Happy Birthday'
to one of his sisters, although she was many miles away in
the UK. On Wednesdays Elsie attended a women's prayer

meeting and normally drove herself there in the afternoon, taking other ladies with her. However, on this day John decided to take them to the meeting place as he had a new battery that needed acid, which could be obtained at the aircraft hangar. Four women and four children piled into the Land Rover. Little four-year-old Alyssa sat in the front between Elsie and John, and put her hands on the wheel pretending to help John drive, while he chatted with her. They were a happy group of people, enjoying the company of others. John dropped them off and drove away, promising to be back to collect them after the meeting.

They had only just started the meeting when Will, the mechanic from the hangar, came looking for Elsie. Even before he spoke she realized there was something wrong. 'There's been an accident and John has been hurt,' he said, but couldn't give any details. Arriving at the local hospital Elsie found that John had a broken jaw and collarbone, and other wounds to his head, caused by a steel pipe springing up and ramming through the dashboard of his vehicle as he had left the aircraft hangar. She was relieved that he was conscious, and as she held his hand he said her name, but she knew he was in much pain and advised him not to try and talk. He was given blood and then taken to an operating theatre where a dentist wired his jaw. Elsie then went home for a time, but was soon on her way back to the hospital. She found herself planning the sort of care John would need, and how she would help him to eat. It did not occur to her that she would soon have a much more serious situation to face.

As she waited outside the operating theatre John was brought out – he was unconscious. Elsie now realized that it was possible he had brain damage, but in the midst of her devastation she experienced an amazing sense of peace. Throughout the next few hours Elsie was shown great love and concern by nationals and expatriates. Many came and sat quietly with her and prayed. John did not regain consciousness, and the next day, the 9th March, at 7.30 p.m., he slipped quietly into God's presence. The good soldier of Jesus Christ had endured hardness, but he had fought a good fight, and he had kept the faith. God's appointed time for John to enter His Kingdom had come.

Preparations for John's funeral began early the next morning. Women and girls were out as dawn broke to gather tropical flowers and make beautiful wreathes. Workmen were busy digging John's grave. There were various possibilities for the place of burial – the local chief had offered to open a special piece of land, and the church elders had suggested an honoured place in front of the church. But the third option was the one chosen. John was to be buried among the local people in their common burial ground, quite near to the airstrip from which he had made so many journeys both to places nearby and to distant countries.

Crowds of Africans and expatriates began to gather from near and far. Messages had been sent out by drum beating and by radio, and a fleet of five MAF planes had been used to ferry in some expatriates from centres further away. A radio message of sympathy was sent from Nebobongo, where John and Elsie had worked in the fifties. Later it was learned that at Napopo, a remote AIM centre in the north, a small group of leprosy patients had arranged their own service of thanksgiving for John's life.

A thanksgiving service was the first event of the day. Many crowded into the church, and those who could not get in looked through the windows. The medical staff choir sang and a number of people paid tribute to the influence that John's life had had on theirs. As the coffin was carried to the grave the nursing staff in their white uniforms walked alongside, and hundreds of others followed. Many people had known John primarily as their doctor, but he was also their friend and brother in Christ. He had known so many of them personally, and had prayed with them, advised them and exhorted them. The leprosy patients among them represented those for whom John had worked so tirelessly in Africa, India and Nepal.

As hundreds of people gathered around the grave there were more tributes and joyful singing. In the sadness of bereavement there was a predominant note of triumph, as those grieving knew that although he was absent bodily, John was present with his Lord. After his body had been lowered into the grave, cries of, 'Hallelujah, Hallelujah' rang out over the hillside as the Nyankunde trumpeters played the glorious music of Handel's 'Hallelujah Chorus'.

Epilogue

John's seventy-year-long life had touched so many others, but he was now experiencing the fullness of joy with His Lord and Master. One of his grandchildren summed up his passing perfectly, saying, 'He is having such a lovely time in heaven.'

What legacy did he leave behind? Not much in the way of money or material goods. It didn't take Elsie long to sort out his personal possessions. But as the letters of sympathy poured in from around the world, one tribute especially brought great joy to Elsie's heart. A young pilot came to talk to her. His wife had had a large, non-malignant growth near her mouth. John had taken great care to remove it without leaving a scar. The pilot said he had been planning to give up flying for MAF in Zaire because the pressures had become too great for him. These, and other pressures in his personal life, had caused him to lose his love for Jesus. But then he added, 'Elsie, I want you to know that I have rededicated my life to the Lord because I saw Him so much at work in John's life.'

★ ★ ★ ★ ★

Elsie stayed on at Nyankunde for five months after John's death, in order to tie up all the loose ends and to hand over their work to TLM's new Africa Director, Dr Piet Both, and other TLM staff. Twenty-one years of leprosy work and teaching programmes had resulted in there being a very low incidence of leprosy cases in north-east Zaire. TLM now concentrates its efforts on the Kinshasa and Bukavu areas, with an increasing number of nationals taking leadership positions.

After returning to the UK, Elsie lived with Lois and her family for eleven months before finding a house in Beeston, Nottingham, and enjoys loving support from her family, TLM and Cornerstone Church. While she misses John as much as ever, her five grandchildren are a joy. She now speaks at women's meetings, sometimes on behalf of TLM, and follows TLM's ongoing work in many countries closely.

* * * * *

There is no human answer to the question as to why God allowed John to be involved in such a bizarre accident, and to die from the injuries he received. One of his older sisters, Annette, found in the words of Isaiah 57:1–2 a reassuring reminder of God's sovereignty at every stage of life: 'The righteous perish and no one ponders it in his heart; devout men are taken away, and no one understands that the righteous are taken away to be spared from evil. Those who walk uprightly enter into peace; they find rest as they lie in death.' To Annette, these words seemed to have special significance, as in the year following John's death the conflict worsened in Zaire, resulting in terrible civil war, tribal conflicts and a great deal of suffering. The fighting reached the area around Nyankunde in 1996, and expatriates were advised to leave. There was much looting and damage and a battle took place right on the mission station. People there had to flee to the hills for safety. In 1997 there seemed to be some hope of rebuilding, and a few missionaries were able to return. But the church stood strong throughout the troubles. As God's people rely only on Him through all the turmoil and instability of life in central Africa, the church will continue to shine amid the darkness.

John once remarked to a colleague, 'If you want to find more water, you have to dig deeper.' This simple illustration from African life sums up his tireless energy and seemingly unquenchable thirst for the Lord. John experienced times of heartache and misunderstandings, and the separations from his family sometimes brought criticism from well-meaning friends and relations. However, the testimony of the Psalmist in Psalm 87:7 is 'All my fountains are in you.' Like the Palmist, John knew that there is no other place to seek refreshment than in the Lord. His burning desire was to share that water with others, to encourage them to dig to quench their spiritual thirst and to experience the power of God.

The command of Jesus Christ to go and make disciples of all nations has not been rescinded. But we cannot close our eyes to the fact that the world is changing rapidly. No longer is Europe the centre for the expansion of Gospel outreach. There is tremendous growth in many churches of the non-Western world. The frontiers of mission are changing, and we have to be open to new ways of sharing the good news. Christians may enter countries that are closed to missionaries to undertake secular jobs. These

Christians are just as much involved as witnesses as are those who can still be termed missionaries.

But the biblical principles of service for Christ remain unchanged. John was single-minded for God's glory and for His Kingdom. God's grace made it possible for him to fulfil the commitment he made. Every Christian is called to walk in this way, whether for service in our own culture or somewhere else. We miss out immeasurably if we choose to take an easier path. It is no risky venture to take the path of full dedication, because the Lord who calls us is the same Lord who goes with us. As 1 Thessalonians 5:24 assures us, 'The One who calls you is faithful.'